Leap Year

at

The Coffee Shop

Red San Publishing

PO BOX 284, Bellevue, Washington, U.S.A.

www.redsanpublishing.com

First published in 2011 by Red San Publishing.

Library of Congress Control Number (LCCNs): 2011926452

Leap Year at the Coffee Shop/Michael L. Eads—1st ed.

eBook: ISBN-13: 978-0-9798484-8-3 ISBN-10: 0-9798484-8-2
Paperback: ISBN-13: 978-0-9834500-0-9 ISBN-10: 0-9834500-0-5

Designed by Bing Yang

Printed in the United States of America

2 4 6 8 10 9 7 5 3 1

To Laura and baby Joel

LEAP YEAR AT THE COFFEE SHOP

Michael Louis Eads

Red San Publishing

Seattle, Washington

Let the extra day fall on the shortest month, February, to balance the riddle of time.

— *Unknown*

CONTENTS

PROLOGUE

I T WAS AN OLD STYLE COFFEE SHOP, a blend of European elegance and the Seattle grunge scene. Although grunge music had lost some of its appeal, this was still Seattle where coffee and music meant more to its citizens than almost anywhere else. It was this distinct mixture that attracted people to the coffee shop: Coming in out of the cold on a rainy, late-winter, gray, blah day and sitting down with a hot cup of coffee meant more here. Just holding a hot cup between your cold hands and sipping that enticing brew made only the way baristas in Seattle could, meant more. Hands warmed and palates sweetened; making the coffee shop feel like home.

This is where Mitch Lucas was most at ease. He loved his home, but sometimes it was hard to go there, knowing no one was waiting. Knowing he would be alone: His reward the next day?—the same thing. It wasn't so bad because Mitch loved life and his own company; preferred it over the company of strangers or even the few friends he had. His father told him long ago, "You'll be lucky if you have four or five real friends your whole life." Gone now, Dad must have known something he just wouldn't or couldn't tell his son. Mitch somehow sensed he would spend most of his life alone. Difficult to put into words, just a feeling he had.

But at the coffee shop Mitch was a different man; someone who belonged, someone anyone could talk to. Maybe the way the coffee shop looked made him feel at ease. It looked nothing like his dark, but impeccably kept home. From the street it resembled an old weathered Seattle house with a steep-pitched roof. The rippled, large-squared, dark-brown siding gave it a nostalgic flavor. The out-of-place coffee shop rested on a busy street-corner between a drugstore on one side and a salon on the other.

Inside it was well-lighted with windows everywhere. Some were stained-glass with patterns that resembled wavy lines of a multicolored cornfield. When the sun penetrated through windblown flickering branches on the leafless trees in late winter, the windows came alive. Mitch was convinced he was the only one who noticed it.

Mitch was convinced he was the only one to distinguish a lot of things he laid eyes on. He'd proven it many times while in a crowded room; pointing out something no one else could see. A gift he acquired from his father. One he was proud of. Shiny hardwood maple floors, multi-colored walls and a spiral staircase (made from different shades of mahogany and oak) led up to a tiny room with a red plastic table. A bench up there enticed young couples to make-out, so Mitch rarely went up the spiral staircase. Besides, he hated that plastic table and wanted to smash it with a sledgehammer. It was this accumulation of oddities that gave the coffee shop its character.

THE COFFEE SHOP had everything he liked. And the coffee; let's just say Mitch took pleasure in his only real vice, indulging whenever he could. All the coffee girls knew how he liked it. Mitch could not disguise his happy face at the coffee shop. He belonged there.

This is also where Mitch heard a hundred different stories from almost as many people. Unfortunately, most of the stories were dull and contrived. Mitch detested liars, yet he always seemed to catch people in lies. He didn't care about trivial canards, everyone told those. It was deliberate deceit that got under his skin.

On February 29th in a leap year, Mitch shook hands with destiny. An extra ¼ day left over each year that added up to one day out of every four. A day mankind needed to balance the books after he discovered the passage of time.

On a blustery, rainy day he was privileged to listen to the most genuine and peculiar stories he ever heard. Divine intervention or quirk of fate?—He didn't know. Come in out of the cold, where it's warm, to Mitch's favorite coffee shop and eavesdrop.

ONE

MITCH'S SUPERPOWERS

F ROM THE TIME HE WAS A LITTLE BOY MITCH WANTED to do something incredible—something *no one* else had done. He wanted superpowers. Almost every boy wanted superpowers, inspired by comic books and TV shows of the day. Men were walking on the moon and in America, anything seemed possible.

Mitch was full of exuberance and peculiar ambition for such a young boy. He *was* different—handsome with lots of girlfriends. They said he was cute.

Mitch hated that—no one with superpowers should be cute. He had dirty-blond hair, high cheek-bones and a distinctive crooked smile. Quite the ladies' man at such a young age. But he knew this would not be his destiny. Adult life would be completely different than his youth. The cute face would fade. The inno-cent smile would slowly vanish and give way to the numbing normality of grown-up life. Boyhood charm could not last.

GROWING UP IN Seattle, Washington, Mitch attended Saint Luke's Catholic school. The girls were pretty and sweet. The boys were rough and mean. He soon realized—get tough or get out!

Every day at recess the boys would play a fast game of dodge ball or what the Catholic boys affectionately called 'Soak 'em.' They used six red-rubber-balls about the size of volleyball. That ball stung like hell when it hit you. Object of the game: Face each other with a five-boy-limit on each team and try to hit one other with those red-rubber-balls until the opposing team was annihilated. The team with the most boys standing when the recess whistle blew was the winner. The team with fewest boys standing lost.

A scrimmage line was established; usually a line in the old weathered playground pavement. A few dark-blue sweaters (these were required as part of the Catholic uniform) were quickly discarded and used as boundary lines. Three balls were placed on each side of the scrimmage line. Then someone yelled: 'READY-SET-GO!' The best throwers on each side scrambled for the balls to throw as hard as they could at their opponents. Just *kill* 'em all!

In Mitch's class there were twenty boys and you did not *dare* skip out of any game for fear of being labeled a coward the rest of your kid life. In Catholic school that's about the same amount of time you spent in hell, *eternity*. If you got hit with a ball, you had to go to jail and wait. Everyone hated to go to jail because all you could do was look at the backsides of your team and watch them, helplessly.

Mitch made up his mind early in this crazy game he would not spend time in jail. *Jail* was for losers! By the time he made it to third grade, just eight years old; he'd mastered catching the ball. See, catching the ball allowed one of your teammates to be released from jail. And Mitch could catch that red-rubber-ball better than *anyone* at school. Everyone wanted him on their team. This also made Mitch a huge target. Every boy in school wanted to put him in jail, but few ever did. They aimed for his face and genitals, throwing the ball as hard as they could. Mitch could catch the ball against his stomach, in front of his face, over his head, and even down by his shoes like a basket catch.

Mitch's catching skills were so exceptional the entire school agreed any opposing thrower would not be sent to jail simply because *he* caught a ball. A player would only be allowed to get out of jail (on his team) if Mitch caught the ball. And he almost always did.

This caused a major uproar on Saint Luke's playground. It gave Mitch demigod status, which he detested strongly. It also made it unfair for any team he played on. But that did not stop the other boys—they *wanted* to be on Mitch's team because he *always* found a way to win.

11

To end upheaval it was decided *all* throwers who threw a ball at any opposing players on *any* team would be allowed to stay in the game if the opposing player caught the ball. Someone would still be allowed to get out of jail on the catcher's team but the thrower could stay in the game. A rule change initiated by the skills of one player. This made the game brutal because it forced the boys to throw balls harder. Only the fast and tough could survive. This crazy game called *dodge ball* was played a thousand different ways on a thousand different playgrounds, but at Saint Luke's Catholic school a major rule had been changed because of *one* player, Mitch Lucas.

Through general consensus the boys at school had disallowed using the ball to deflect other incoming balls. They only had ten minutes each recess period and twenty minutes during lunch period to play the game they loved. They quickly found out if everyone tried to block the ball, the games would drag on too long for any team to have time to win. Besides, trying to block a ball (especially in Mitch's mind) was for wimps.

Any ball thrown at your opponents from the shoulders up was supposed to be illegal. But Saint Luke's was a rough Catholic school so no one enforced that stupid rule. Mitch had found his *first* superpower. He was fast, tough and respected. At the school he attended in the late sixties and early seventies, *respect* meant acceptance. And being accepted meant you belonged. Mitch spent his entire adult life defiant—unwilling to conform to anyone or anything. At Saint Luke's he was just an awkward boy, desperate to fit in.

BY THE FALL of fifth grade, word got out Mitch was the best player at school. This enraged the other kids. Mitch didn't want to be singled out as the best player because he knew what it meant—every kid in school trying to gun him down. It was decided; a showdown between the top players in the fifth and sixth grade would happen after school, the Wednesday before the four-day-break for Thanksgiving. Mitch was nervous, the whole school would be watching—even the nuns, who he was sure, had it in for him because of his newfound popularity. Vanity, after all, is a sin.

Three players were picked out of three-hundred twenty-five boys in sixteen classes with a three-player limit from each class; almost fifty of the best fifth and sixth graders. Naturally, you wanted to pick the best catcher first, followed by the boy who could throw the hardest and hit what he aimed at. Mitch could do both. His incredible catching skills had overshadowed his formidable throwing ability.

Each class took a vote on who would represent them. Mitch got every vote but one. Later he found out it was a pretty girl named Susan, who once had a huge crush on him. The crush faded so her vote was "No." She cast a vote to her current flame, Billy, who ironically was picked as one of the best throwers. This was a poor decision from the class. Billy was good but nowhere near the best. Mitch made it clear that Ray— one of the toughest kids at school should be on the team. Ray could throw *hard*, hit what he was aiming at, and like Mitch, never backed down in the heat of battle.

The last choice was Marty. Marty was Mitch's best friend but probably the worst player in class. Everyone loved Marty, even the nuns. The model Catholic boy who had everyone fooled but Mitch. Majority ruled and Mitch, Marty and Billy would represent their class. Mitch told Ray he would find a way to get him on the team. *Marty*, on his team—no fucking way.

Mitch was the youngest of five kids and everyone at home were talking about the game. His sisters were already in high school and thought the whole thing was silly. Only one of his brothers, Dean, one year older, who went to the same school, said he would be there to watch. Dean liked to play basketball and baseball, but not much else. His oldest brother Paul, (four years older) questioned Mitch's abilities as a player. "I don't think he's so special, I could get him out with one throw." Typical older brother Mitch thought, they're all legends in their own minds. "I don't care what you think Paul, I don't care what any of you think, I'm gonna go out there and win."

"Relax son," his dad said, tucking in a neatly pressed white long-sleeved shirt, ready to go to work, "I'm sure you'll do fine."

"Thanks Dad," Mitch said looking at Paul with his tongue extended all the way. "Just remember one thing son," (oh God the dreaded catch line Mitch thought) "there's always somebody better."

"No one at school is better than me!" Mitch shouted.

The morning of the game Mitch was up early to prepare his project for science class. It was still dark outside but soon the crisp, clear, cold morning would give way to a rare brilliant sunny November day. The class's assignment: collect as many different varieties of leaves as a curious fifth-grader could. Mitch hated homework, but this was something you could do *outside* in the rain. He loved the rain, but could not understand why some kids would just go home when the weather turned bad. He gathered every leaf he could get his hands on; easy to do in late November. His mother gave him an empty milk bottle made of thick glass so shiny it looked brand new. Mitch carefully folded each leaf and squeezed it through the narrow top. The idea: lay the bottle flat during the demonstration to display his masterpiece. He put in some moist dirt to give the milk bottle an earthy effect. It worked; the leaves were all still moist and opened slowly as they dried inside the bottle. Mitch took it to his mother for one last seal of approval.

"Whatever you do, don't drop it Mitchell, you've worked so hard on it."

"Great," Mitch thought, "now I will think about *not* dropping it all the way to school."

Every morning before school Mitch would cut through the back-yard gate into the alley. This could be risky because *the alley* was where kids from public school hung out and sometimes picked on him. That was usually after school because public school kids got up after *and* got out of school earlier than Catholic kids.

Mitch was in a good mood staring at the shiny glass bottle full of leaves. He wore gloves that frigid morning holding onto the bottle tightly with both hands. Daybreak revealed a late-November sky that resembled burnt ambers over the Cascade Mountains. His hands were sweating through the gloves. The milk bottle slipped right out of them. He watched the bottle fall to the ground in slow motion. This wasn't happening! Reality set in when Mitch heard the un-mistakable sound of glass hit the pavement.

"There goes my science project," he said dazed. "What am I gonna tell my teacher, my friends, oh God, what the hell am I going to say to Mom?!"

Feeling sorry for himself, he looked at the shat-tered bottle, shards of glass glistening in the morning light. Then Mother Nature wielded her cruel side. A sudden, powerful gust of wind funneled through the alleyway and took Mitch's dream. One maple leaf trapped under some dirt and glass was all that re-mained. *"I hate you God"* was the last thing Mitch said as he hung his head down and went to school.

WHEN HE ARRIVED at school Mitch's agony was obvious to everyone. "*What's the matter Mitch, ya ready for the big game?*"

It was the day before Thanksgiving with the biggest game in his life that afternoon, but Mitch didn't care. All the kids from his science class were supposed to drop off their projects before school. When Mitch walked in and saw other kids' displays he didn't feel so bad. They were so cool. Joseph, the smartest kid in class, used an old style Christmas calendar tree made from velvet. It had pockets that represented the twelve days of Christmas. He changed the calendar into a Thanksgiving theme and put a different leaf in each pocket. Mitch said, "That's the neatest thing I've ever seen, you'll win for sure Joseph."

"Thanks Mitch, so where's your project?"

"*Broken and blown away somewhere in the alley by my house,*" Mitch said embarrassed.

"Jeez Mitch, how'd that happen?"

"I dropped the milk bottle and now I'm screwed."

"What about the game, aren't you excited?"

"I don't give a damn about that stupid game right now; I'm so goddamn mad I broke that bottle! Now I got to face Mrs. Riemann, what am I supposed to tell *her*?"

"Tell the truth," Joseph said innocently. That's the thing Mitch admired about Joe, he still trusted people. A straight-A student and probably the smartest kid in school, but to Mitch he was the most naïve kid he knew. How could someone so smart be so stupid?

17

You *never* told the truth at Catholic school. Mitch tried it one time and got the shit slapped out of him three different times from *three* different people—just for telling the truth. After that he never trusted any nuns at school. He would rather suffer the consequences of lying as a sin to God than be persecuted for telling the truth and taking the blame for something he did not do. The one lesson Mitch learned early at Catholic school is life is *cruel* and almost always unfair. Mitch wasn't the only kid who felt that way, for many kids, Catholic school was a hopeless situation.

Mitch avoided Mrs. Riemann as long as he could. She finally came around and politely asked, "Where is your project Mitchy boy?" His Catholic defense mechanism was on auto-drive.

"Well you see Mrs. Riemann; I was on my way to school and those public school boys saw me carrying a glass milk bottle full of leaves. Anyway, there was a scuffle and they broke my bottle and kicked all my leaves away." Mitch was surprised; his lying abilities had improved.

"Are you okay, Mitchy boy?" she said stroking his dirty blond hair while looking at him like the son she never had. "I'm fine Mrs. Riemann; just a little shook up is all." Mitch was amazed at his *complete* lack of guilt after telling such a blatant lie. "Those unruly public school boys, something should be done about them." Mrs. Riemann turned her attention to Joseph. He did not say a word. He knew if he did Mitch would pound him good. Mitch didn't want that, he really liked Joe. Mrs. Riemann bought it and told all the other kids to stay away from those *ungodly* public school boys.

The rest of Mitch's school day went pretty well. He was satisfied with his improved lying skills. After such a crazy morning he was amazed how calm he was. Besides, one lie was as good as another and they all lead Mitch to one place: HELL! Fine with him, that was a lot better than sitting around playing a harp in the clouds forever. "*Jesus*, heaven sounded boring," Mitch would think to himself at Mass. It was almost three o'clock and time for the biggest game in his life. Suddenly, he wanted to go home. He could no longer fake it—he was terrified.

WHEN MITCH WALKED on to the playground that after-noon it looked different. The shortest days of the year were here and the sun was already low on the horizon. The golden rays reflecting off the old weathered brick school created an ancient backdrop. It resembled an old Roman Coliseum where athletes gathered to battle. Mitch realized why it looked different—he was usually home by now. Every kid should have been home, but they were not. They all showed up to witness this epic event. Mitch looked around and said, *"I'm the best player at school and today I'm gonna prove it."*

Father Henry organized everything and told all the

boys to come together. He announced *he* would be the referee. That was fine with most of the boys; Father Henry was an *"old school"* priest, strict but fair. He liked Mitch, used to always tell him he was a tough kid, like he was in the old days. Father Henry could also be very intimidating; six-foot-tall and at least two-hundred pounds. He had black hair; slicked-back with what resembled Vaseline it was so thick. He wore dark-rimmed glasses with thick lenses that intensified his unforgettable glare when angered. It was understood by every kid at school, a given, you did not want to make Father Henry mad.

The teams were set: eight teams with five-players on each were to compete in a round-robin elimination tournament. Father Henry intentionally interspersed players from other classes and different grades. Mitch didn't care about the sixth-graders because he was better than any of them. He understood what Father Henry was trying to do—get kids that normally play against each other to play *with* each other. Only the three players selected from each class would be guaranteed to play on *their* respective teams.

Almost all the kids showed up so Father Henry could rotate a player in if another got tired or hurt. It was a good idea because in dodge ball you might not get hurt, but you would certainly get tired. The goal of the contest was simple: last team standing wins. Mitch realized his chances with the team Father Henry had picked for him were not so good. Ironically, Ray, the kid Mitch stood up for, was on his team. Mitch made good on his word.

A few selected kids, including Billy, did not show up. Father Henry made it clear to everyone including the nuns that Ray belonged on the team. Nevertheless, Mitch saw that the other players on his team were a little better than average at best. Other teams had a more balanced array of good throwers and catchers. Mitch walked up to Ray, "I'm glad you're here Ray, without you we have no chance of winning." Mitch noticed Ray's chest puff out and saw a look of pride in his face. Not a big talker, Ray said, "Thanks Mitch, I won't let you down."

Father Henry got everyone's attention by blowing the recess whistle. He explained the rules and what he expected: *"I want a fair, but competitive game from every boy here. I expect you all to do your best. However, I must warn you, I will not tolerate any name-calling, unnecessary roughhousing or unsportsman-like conduct. If you do, you're out, no exceptions!"* His sermon put the fear of God into every kid at Saint Luke's.

Mitch's team was selected first to play. He and Ray were ready. Their opponents: a team that had some good players, but Mitch knew his team could take 'em. They had a kid who *thought* he was the best player in school. A sixth-grader named Andy Richards. Mitch hated his guts and couldn't wait to hit him in the face with that red-rubber-ball. Father Henry blew the whistle. The games commenced. Andy's team avoided Mitch and Ray and proceeded to knock out

Marty with their first throw, then two other players in less than a minute.

"Great," Mitch thought, "we're gonna get knocked out in the first round." They kept throwing the ball at Ray—real hard. Ray was too fast and dodged each throw. Andy wound up and heaved it right at Mitch's face as hard as he could. Mitch dodged it, didn't like it. Ray slapped him on the back, "Nice dodge Mitch."

"Thanks, Ray, let's cream these punks."

Ray got a ball and hit one of their players on the leg, four on two now. Andy the ball-hog wound up again. This time he made a huge mistake. He threw it right at Mitch's stomach and watched as the ball bounced off Mitch's bread-basket and land in-between his forearms.

"Lucky catch Mitch," Andy said as he looked over and pretended not to be scared. Mitch set a clear example to all watching. It wasn't that he caught the ball, everyone expected that. It was the *way* he caught the ball—letting it bounce off his stomach, and then closing his arms around it with the reflexes of a cat.

Every boy on every team was waiting for their turn to hurl that red-rubber-ball at Mitch, now he had something to think about. Mitch's great catch meant someone could get out of jail. Marty waved his hands. Mitch gave him a nod to get back in the game. Marty paid no attention as he tried to walk over to Mitch and get instructions. He got hit with *two* balls at the same time. Mitch just looked at him and shook his head. "Why is this guy my friend?" Mitch mumbled.

Mitch was furious! He grabbed a ball, wound up like a major league pitcher and hit Andy in the same spot he had hit him—right in the stomach. He threw the ball so hard Andy started to cry: "DOESN'T FEEL SO GOOD. DOES IT?!" Mitch yelled. "I hope your team loses Mitch, I hate you." Andy said composing himself just enough through sniffling and tears.

"Ah go home and help your Mamma cook that bird," Mitch retorted with a cool smirk.

"Did you forget what I said Mitch?" Father Henry reminded him. "Sorry Father, it won't happen again." Mitch knew how much he liked him and didn't want to test his patience. "See that it doesn't Mitchy boy."

Mitch and Ray looked over and saw fear in their opponents' eyes. The other team had the advantage, but you wouldn't know it from looking at them. Mitch got a ball, wound up and knocked out another. The other teams watched and realized how good a thrower Mitch was and looked worried. Even one of the nuns said, "That Mitchy is almost as good a thrower as he is a catcher." Mitch and Ray mowed 'em down and the whistle blew. "First game goes to Mitch Lucas's team," Father Henry said smiling. Mitch and Ray hugged each other and went to get some water. They had to get back quick, more kids to kill.

THE ROUND-ROBIN MATCH went on with more of the same. With Ray *and* Mitch's hard, accurate throws and Mitch's magical catches, the other teams crumbled. This made the other players on their team a little jealous. They had five boys on the team and it seemed like only two were playing. Jeff, who was a good at dodging, but nothing else, wanted the ball more. Steve, who wore glasses and couldn't see the ball until it was too late, got knocked out at the worst time. And Marty, well, let's just say no one knows how he made the team. Mitch believed the nuns somehow got him on his team. Ray shouted at them: "SHUT-UP, ANY ONE OF YA SCREWS THIS UP FOR MITCH AND ME, I'LL POUND THE SHIT OUTTA YA! GOT IT! BESIDES IF IT WASN'T FOR MITCH YOU'D ALL BE STUCK IN JAIL SO QUIT WHINING!" That scared 'em good.

Ray could be mean; he *looked* mean, and tough. Mitch was scared of him, but would not let Ray know that. Mitch settled everyone down and told them they could win this thing, but they had to hurry. Marty finally spoke up and said, "Hurry, *why* do we need to hurry?"

"Because Father Henry's gonna stop this thing when it gets dark and that's in a half an hour. "HOLY SHIT!" Ray shouted, "We need to hurry up and win." With the last two teams set it was time for a showdown....

It was Mitch Lucas's team vs. Buster Crooks' team. Buster had the exclusive distinction of being the fastest kid in school. He was a fifth-grader same as Mitch and Ray, but could whip any sixth-grader easy. And he was the best catcher at school other than Mitch. The thing that set Buster apart from every other player, including Mitch, was his dodging ability. He was as graceful on the field as any kid in school and almost impossible to hit with the ball.

He didn't like Mitch much, in fact, he didn't like *anyone* that much. He always walked around with a big grin as if to say, "*I'm the fastest kid in school and I'll prove it anytime, anywhere.*" Mitch and Ray knew this would be their toughest game ever. Ray told Mitch he was gonna try to get him out early and end it. Buster scared Mitch 'cause when they would race he would look over at Mitch halfway through and smile, then hit the rocket thrusters and leave him in the dust. Buster had the superpower every kid wanted, *blazing speed.*

AT EXACTLY FOUR-THIRTY-FIVE PM the two best teams towed the line. The dark grayish-blue twilight reflecting off the school-ground pavement started to give way to the artificial yellow light cast slantwise from the streetlights. They were too far away to keep the game going after dark. The boys were running out of time. Father Henry said: "Better hurry boys. I'm gonna call this off at dark." He blew the whistle; Ray grabbed a ball and threw it right at Buster's head as hard as he could. Buster waited until the ball came within a few feet and then ducked at the last second. "YOU COULDN'T HIT THE SIDE OF THIS SCHOOL WITH THAT BALL!" He shouted over at Ray. Now Ray was incensed. Father Henry told Buster to watch his mouth. "Sorry Father," Buster said with a coy look.

Ray got a ball and unloaded. He hit a kid right in the crotch and he started to cry. Suddenly, Buster wasn't laughing. Ray got a ball back and gunned it at Buster. It was a good throw—*low* and *hard*. Buster swooped down with legs spread and arms low. The ball thumped into his forearms as he coiled them up and clamped down. This allowed the lone boy on Buster's team 'in jail' to be set free. It was now five on five again with the two best players at school facing each other. Buster and Mitch exchanged glares. After seeing that catch, legs spread, arms low and then coiling up to snatch the ball—Mitch wondered if he *was* the best player at school. Buster Crooks looked *unstoppable*.

A kid on Buster's team, Cliff, slow, but a hard thrower got Jeff out; five on four now. Balls were flying and Mitch was getting tired. Buster looked fresh and fast. Mitch wondered, "Does this guy ever get tired?" Steve got a ball and surprised everyone when he went right up near the scrimmage line and heaved it. Another kid on Buster's team turned his head (a fatal mistake) and the ball hit him right in the chest. Four on four now. Steve was too close to the scrimmage line and was creamed with two balls. "Jeez Steve, you can't stay up there."

"I know, I know, sorry Mitch." Four on three— advantage Buster Crooks' team.

Somehow Marty managed to stay in the game.

Mitch hadn't noticed he'd been too locked in on Buster. Buster's team had four players and Mitch knew Marty, Ray or maybe even he would be knocked out soon. Cliff hit Marty right on the butt. "Sorry Mitch, I did the best I could."

"Don't sweat it Marty, you played a great game." It wasn't true, but Marty tried as hard as he could. Right after that Buster hit Ray so hard in the stomach he knocked the wind out him. Ray was okay and Father Henry helped him up and off the field. Mitch was *alone.*

Mitch looked over and saw all four boys staring him down. A boy on Buster's team, Chris Jensen, started to get a little cocky and called Mitch a god-damn-faggot-loser. Calling Mitch Lucas a faggot was bad enough. Calling him a loser was stupid. He walked past the scrimmage line right at Chris with arms down and both fists clenched. Father Henry stopped him just in time and told him to go back over to his side of the playing field. Chris Jensen's face was white with fear.

Father Henry kicked Chris out of the game. "Let me tell you something boy, you're lucky I don't take you upstairs right now and paddle your behind good. It's a good thing I stopped Mitch because he would've carved you up like a Thanksgiving turkey, and if it was up to me I would let 'em. But we have a game to finish so you better just go home before I call your dad and see what *he* thinks about that mouth of yours." Chris *begged* Father Henry not to do that.

Mitch collected himself and told Father Henry he wanted to finish the game. Father Henry made Chris apologize to Mitch. They reluctantly shook hands and then Chris walked off the field just glad he would not have a spanking waiting when he got home. He was the only boy to get ejected that day.

Father Henry told Mitch later the real reason he kicked Chris out was because he called Mitch a loser. That and taking the lord's name in vain. Mitch told Father Henry he was glad he stopped him. "I know it may be a sin Father, but I was ready to pound him good."

"I wouldn't blame ya Mitchy boy, I wouldn't blame ya."

Buster raised a hand for a time out. Mitch knew his strategy, stall as long as he could and wait for Father Henry to call the game. It was four-forty-five and if Father Henry called the game now, Buster's team would win because he had three and Mitch was only *one*.

Mitch was alone and it was almost dark. It was Buster Crooks, Cliff Hendrix and Mark Johnson versus a lone Mitch Lucas. Four of the best players at school, but three were on the other side, facing Mitch. Buster's strategy: throw all three balls at Mitch at the same time. He couldn't dodge them *all*. The two teams towed the scrimmage line. Father Henry placed one ball on Mitch's side and three on the other. The whistle blew and Mitch got to a ball first. He surprised everyone when he didn't move from the center line and gently lobbed the ball under hand, right off Mark's shin. Mark was out.

Buster and Cliff saw a chance and threw their balls at the same time; one came in from the left and another from the right. Mitch realized he couldn't dodge *both* balls so he thrust his pelvis forward as far and fast as he could while still concentrating on Cliff's throw from only ten feet away. It worked. Buster's throw missed him altogether while Cliff's throw came in chest high—the hardest throw to catch because of the rebound effect. The ball would simply bounce away before you had a chance to catch it. Nevertheless this was Mitch Lucas and he had mastered that catch in the third grade. He turned toward Cliff and the ball bounced off his chest then into his tightly clasped extended hands—the catch of his life. Everyone cheered except the other team. Even the callous nuns cheered for Mitch. Was God on his side? All preconceived notions of divine intervention vanished when Mitch looked over at Buster and saw that cocky smile. It looked like God would sit this one out. There was just a hint of daylight.

This allowed one player out of jail. No one said anything on Mitch's team when Ray decided he would be the one to be let out. Mitch let out a deep breath he had been holding for this moment. Ray was mad and everyone could see it. Sensing his hostility or maybe just wanting to calm him down, Mitch called for a timeout. "Make it quick Mitchy boy because you only have a few minutes before dark."

"Yes Sir Father Henry, I will." Father Henry smiled and nodded his approval.

"Listen Ray, I've got an idea."

"Jesus Mitch, hurry up and tell me it's gonna get dark soon and I want to kill these guys."

"Yeah, yeah, I know, so do I, but this isn't the time for stupid mistakes so we gotta make a plan." Ray rolled his eyes, but was curious what Mitch had in mind. "When Father Henry blows the whistle, run to the back out-of-bounds line and stay there. I will stay up near the front and try to get them to throw at me. If we can get one more guy out of jail, I'm sure we'll win. Besides, you can throw harder than me so you might be able to get Cliff out from back there. Remember, he's kinda slow and can't catch very well. And if they do try to throw at you, you should definitely be able to catch it from back there."

"Holy shit Mitch, that's a great idea, let's do it!"

The four boys towed the line, two on each side. Father Henry blew the whistle again. This time, Cliff surprised everyone when he got to a ball first. Ray grabbed a ball and did precisely what Mitch told him not to do—he stayed up front where things can go wrong quickly, and did. Ray and Cliff wound up and threw their respective balls as hard as they could at each other. Mitch and Buster were so enthralled with what was happening they just stood there and watched. Both red-rubber-balls hit their opponents in the stomach at the same time—like two coiled rattle-snakes that struck each other at precisely the right instant. The problem: neither of them caught it. Cliff and Ray walked off the field while Buster and Mitch just looked at each other.

IT SEEMED SOMETHING preordained to have the two best players in school face each other. This wasn't about the teams anymore; it was about these two boys unwilling to give in to the other. Father Henry realized more than anyone what was happening. He could leave these two out there all night and neither one would *ever* quit.

Mitch and Buster exchanged some potent throws and showed all watching why they call it, "dodge ball." Both afraid they would make the fatal mistake—drop the ball. The pale playground lights blinked intermittently until they finally came on when Father Henry blew the whistle and yelled, "GAME OVER!" Mitch and Buster met each other at the scrimmage line and shook hands. "Great game Mitch," Buster said with a smile. "You too Buster, I knew it would come down to us."

Mitch and Buster looked around and noticed almost no one had gone home. They all stayed to watch and they were all cheering. One of the few to go home was Mitch's brother, Dean, whose excuse was, "It was boring." Father Henry approached the last boys standing and put one arm around each. "I want you both to know you played one heck of a game. If you show that kind of guts and determination in life, you will go far." Father Henry blew the whistle one last time and told everyone to go home. "HAVE A GREAT THANKSGIVING EVERYONE AND REMEMBER TO GIVE THANKS TO THE ALMIGHTY WHO GAVE YOU ALL LIFE!" Mitch always appreciated Father Henry's sincerity and the way he made him feel that day—the best day of his life.

FULL OF JOY, Mitch raced home. His mind filled with new emotions. He couldn't remember a time he was more satisfied. He didn't win and he didn't care. He gave it *everything* he had: Only a ten-year-old kid, but almost a man. He skipped home, singing and whis-tling. "Jesus, I must've been daydreaming, how'd I get here?" Mitch had lost track of time and where he was going. He was almost at the cemetery. He'd been here many times before, but always with his older brothers. This time he was *alone* and it was dark.

From atop a hill where he stood he could see the rectangular shaped graveyard. Streetlights approxi-mately every two-hundred feet bordered the entire perimeter and beamed down their bright yellow hue. "That doesn't seem so scary, look at all those lights." Mitch was too happy to be scared and took the long way home around the cemetery. Walking on the side-walk he noticed in between each street light about a twenty-foot gap of total darkness. The huge willows in the shape of giant dark umbrellas whistled in the breeze. He walked into the dark as the wind picked up. In the dark he got scared. He walked out of the dark into the light and the wind blew harder. Now he *wasn't* afraid. Mitch Lucas walked around that cemetery from the light into the shadows until he realized there was *nothing* to be afraid of. "This is stupid, being afraid of the dark, being afraid of this stupid cemetery and all these dead people. I'M NOT AFRAID ANYMORE, YOU HEAR ME CEMETERY, YOU HEAR ME YOU STUPID DEAD PEOPLE, I'M NOT AFRAID!"

Mitch changed that night. *How* or *why* wasn't important. This was the best day of his life. That's why he wasn't afraid anymore. He understood his greatest superpower—he wasn't a quitter. He did not know how to quit. Later in life this unique quality would serve him better than *all* other superpowers combined. But he wasn't alone; Buster Crooks wasn't a quitter either. Father Henry was right; they would've stood there all night throwing those red balls at each other. Mitch understood Buster after that game. They were connected. They never became friends, but had new-found respect for each other that would last the rest of their lives. Mitch was happy to be alive.

GOOD THINGS NEVER last, especially when you're a kid. Dad got transferred to Kansas City, Missouri for a job promotion. This ended Mitch's tenure at Catholic school. From now on, it was public school. He did not feel accepted at public school—just couldn't seem to fit in. He loved sports and tried just about everything growing up. He tried out for baseball, football, basketball and track. Mitch was fast, but the track coach caught him smoking one day behind the storage shed and kicked him off the team. On a dare from high school buddies he tried boxing at the local Boys Club. He loved boxing, but just didn't like seeing his own blood spilled on the canvas, or the dried blood of all the warriors who had left their dark-red stains of pride for every other fighter to see. However, Mitch was stubborn and his inability to quit made him susceptible to more powerful punchers. He could take a hard punch, but after two years he decided to hang up the gloves. He would brag later that boxing was the hardest three minutes in *any* sport.

As the years went by he lost interest in sports and fell in with the wrong crowd. He already smoked cigarettes, but now he was also drinking and partying until daybreak. He started smoking pot because almost everyone he knew either had it or knew where to get it. Getting stoned with friends made him feel he *belonged*. He could break the law and *rules* at the same time. Mitch *hated* rules. In high school he cut so many classes during his sophomore and junior years his guidance counselor told him to *consider* dropping out.

Somehow, he managed to squeak by and graduate with exactly thirty-two credits. Mitch's way not to follow the crowd was to hang out with the *wrong* crowd. Defiant of his father, yet knowing Dad was right all along; Mitch was trapped between doing what society had told him was right and rebelling against mindless conformity. Later in life he realized drugs were just another way of trying to fit in with something that did not exist. It took a long time for him to admit his *drug years* were a mistake.

HIS FAMILY SPENT eighteen months in Kansas City before returning back home to Seattle. Dad hated the new job and the god-awful heat. Their first day there it was 102°. It was early July with the hottest days of summer still to come. Mitch and his siblings spent every available minute at the pool. On the days when it wasn't so hot, say under ninety, he would play tennis or a pickup game of football with his older brothers and friends. Again, his catching abilities got him picked early on when choosing sides. Sometimes even before his older brothers, which irked them a little. He was still popular with the girls, especially around the pool. As it turned out this would be the only time in his life he felt comfortable around the opposite sex.

One hot August day about a year after they moved to Kansas City, the most popular and beautiful girl in the sixth grade, Joyce Allen, showed up at the pool. It was weird because Mitch never saw her there before or after that day. She wore a vanilla colored two-piece bikini that looked better than ice cream next to her long, wavy black hair and dark-tanned skin. Just twelve years old, but she had the figure of a girl *much* older. Even Mitch's oldest brother Paul wanted to know who she was. Every boy around Mitch's age and older lusted for her. Just to *look* at her on that hot

August day made you feel alive.

Mitch liked the way Joyce looked, but did not care for her personality. She acted a little snobby to him at school. She was snobby to *all* boys at school. Beautiful, popular and smart—how could she not be conceited? Mitch did not know why he liked her in spite of this, except to say a beautiful face and body can make up for almost any character flaws.

All the boys started diving off the board and showing off. The pool became crowded and choppy. Mitch just sat in the shallow end near the steps kicking his legs back and forth in the water. The goddess walked down the steps right in front of him.

She tilted her head back and slowly submerged it until all Mitch could see was her beautiful face and closed eyes just under the ripples. She came up the same way she went under, *slow* and *easy, as* if that hot afternoon would last forever. She tilted her head back down as the water ran down every curve of her body. Then she opened her eyes and smiled at Mitch. She stood about five feet in front of him with the water-line just reaching the top of her belly button. Her wet hair now straight, stuck to her body, covered the white bikini top, but not the important parts. Mitch *tried* not to stare. Mom always said, *"It's rude to stare son."* She *wanted* Mitch to look. He could only manage a quick glance and then look away. She made him nervous. As she started to walk toward him, with every step, Mitch felt time slow down, ready to permanently preserve each indelible image in his memory. How could any boy forget this?

When Joyce finally reached the side of the pool she pulled herself up with those long tanned arms and plopped her butt right next to Mitch's. It took *all* his willpower to pretend he wasn't excited to have her there, *so close.*

"So why aren't *you* diving off the board?"

"Don't feel like it."

"What do you feel like doing Mitch?" Was this a trick question? How in the hell was he supposed to answer that? It was hot, but Mitch was cool. "I don't know. We could do something together if you want to." Joyce smiled and her straight white teeth gleamed in the hot summer sun.

"I know—we could play a game. I'll grab a quarter. We'll throw it in the deep end and then go get it. We could take turns, it'll be fun. Spend the day with me Mitch."

There were times in his life when Mitch believed there was no God, especially when he attended Catholic school. After all, where in the *hell* was God when you needed him?

God must have been smiling down at him that day because the goddess of sixth grade wanted to spend the day with him at *his* pool. All the other boys looked at Joyce and wondered the usual adolescent male preconceived notion, *"what in the hell is she doing with him?"*

Joyce went up to the lifeguard, Dave, a muscle-bound blond guy and the only one around the pool with a darker tan than hers, and asked for a quarter. There was some hesitation until Joyce flashed that pretty smile. Dave acquiesced and reached into his red shorts to hand her a quarter. Even Mitch was surprised.

"What did you say to him? That asshole would never give me anything."

"I just told him the truth. We're gonna play and I would give it back when we're done.

He said he likes you Mitch and you know a lot of tricks underwater."

"I guess that's why he's always kicking me out of here. If I just jump off the diving board wrong or make too big a splash, he tells me I have to go home, doesn't even warn me. My first day here this summer he kicked me out and all I did was push my brother in the pool. That white nosed bum in the sun can go straight to hell. I hate 'em."

"Jeez Mitch, sounds like you've got quite a temper."

"Oh I get it, you like him because he's older and he's got all those muscles and he's a lifeguard and I'm ..."

"You're what?"

"Getting tired of this crap so maybe we should just ..."

"Relax Mitch, I don't like that lifeguard, let's just play and forget him. Show me some underwater tricks."

"I don't know if I want to now." Joyce put a hand on his thigh and Mitch thought he was going to die. "Oh please won't you show me Mitch, *please* ..."

The hot early-August sun heated the concrete to an excruciating burn to bare skin. Mitch kept it bearable by splashing water over his red swim trunks and would run down the lip of the pool deck and where they sat. Joyce splashed Mitch playfully then pushed down with her hands until her butt lifted up just enough to slide down the edge of the pool until her toes touched the bottom. She grabbed Mitch's hands and pulled until he was standing in the shallow end looking into the eyes of pure adolescent seduction.

After a while they forgot who they were. All social preconceived notions of who they *should* be were gone. Just a girl and boy—two kids having fun in the glistening water of the pool.

Mitch showed Joyce every trick he knew, every dive off the board and every underwater move, except one, the entire length of the pool under water in one breath maneuver. For some reason he could not tell her he could do it—that would be bragging. Mitch did not consider it a superpower. Maybe because when he moved underwater near the bottom he felt safe. It was weird. Above water the screams and noise grounded him to the earth. But underwater, he was on another planet, indifferent to the inaudible sounds above. The best memories he had from living in Kansas City were at the bottom of his favorite swimming pool. The best memories, that is, until *now*.

Meanwhile, the other boys taunted Mitch and clamored for Joyce's attention. Mitch was amazed because she ignored them and focused on him. Why she did this remained a mystery. Mitch didn't try to touch her. It wasn't because she was the most beautiful girl at school not to mention as popular as The Beatles. It was something else. Mitch figured Joyce did not want yet another boy, in the incredibly long line of boys who tried to put their hands on her. Joyce took great pleasure throwing the quarter she had charmed out of the lifeguard, and never gave back, in the deepest part of the pool. Then, like an underwater homing pigeon, Mitch would retrieve it, hold up the small round shiny trophy and wait for the goddess' approval. Joyce clapped and laughed as the other boys looked at her with disgust. Why did she ignore them? The truth was she really liked Mitch. Nevertheless, in the soon-to-be social circles of junior-high-school, Mitch was not in her league.

Joyce said her mother would be there at seven to pick her up. It was supper time and the sun now low on the horizon was partially blocked from a nearby hill. The shallow end was now completely *in the shadows*. Mitch and Joyce basked in the early evening 100° sun at the deep end. They were at the opposite end of the pool where Joyce first sat next to Mitch, looking at each other's legs gently moving back and forth underwater. Joyce told Mitch to stand up. Then she reached out her left hand and grabbed his right hand. "Let's jump in at the same time and go down to the bottom, she said." Mitch felt a huge lump it his throat as his heart started pumping.

"Sure that would be fun but can I tell you a trick first?" Joyce was curious. "What trick Mitch?"

"While you're going down to the bottom slowly let the air out of your lungs."

"That sounds hard."

"I know, but it's easy, you just have to relax. If you see too many bubbles you're letting the air out too fast. Remember, small bubbles all the way down to the bottom."

"Okay Mitch, I'll try, but if I run out of air I'm coming right back up."

"You'll be fine Joyce; you just have to trust me."

"I do trust you Mitch, let's do it."

The idea behind letting air out of your lungs is you can stand up (or even lie down flat on your back) at the bottom of the pool. With little or no air in the lungs you're no longer buoyant. You can hang around the bottom until you need air. This is not like holding your breath because there is *little* breath to hold. The tricky part is not letting *all* the air out too fast. Then you're at the bottom with nothing to breathe in, but water. Mitch found out he could let *almost* all the air out of his lungs and walk across the bottom while the remaining air from his lungs trickled bubbles from his mouth to the top of the pool. He discovered this trick on his own and any kid who witnessed it would just look down from the top and marvel. Any kid around Mitch's age that saw him maneuver underwater believed he was either half dolphin or had superpowers. Joyce noticed it too and was impressed—just what Mitch wanted.

Joyce saw her mom walk down from parking lot. Now, she had to hurry. She held Mitch's right hand in her left hand and her nose with the other as they jumped in together. It was twelve feet deep where they jumped in. A lot of kids had gone home for dinner and the only other people in the pool were little kids playing with their parents in the shady shallow end. Their hands immediately unlocked. Joyce reached bottom first because she let the air out of her lungs too fast. Mitch landed a second later. He was only an inch shorter than her but underwater she looked six feet tall—more *beautiful* than ever. Mitch pointed at his mouth to gesture to Joyce she was blowing out too many bubbles. She smiled and the bubbles started to get smaller and smaller ...

They were at the bottom of a chlorine-filled pool with their eyes wide open and didn't care. Joyce pulled Mitch's hands up and over her shoulders. Then with her eyes still open she put her mouth over his. She pulled him close and Mitch forgot where he was, *who* we was. He didn't care about anything anymore, except making this moment last. Could it last?

They held each other tenderly at the bottom while blowing bubbles into each other's mouth. Mitch realized he would be connected to this goddess in some way for the rest of his life. Each bubble felt like some new form of kinetic energy, softly entering his mouth—filling him with her young beautiful essence. Could he already love her?

Suddenly, Joyce unlocked their lips, bent down and pushed up to the shiny waterline with the diving board moving back and forth with the waves. Mitch stood there a few more seconds because he wanted to savor this moment, but the need for air overcame him, and he too ascended as fast as he could to the top. He gasped for air and saw Joyce dry off and put a towel around her waist as she waved goodbye. Before he could say anything she was already getting in her mom's car. Mitch just treaded water knowing he probably would not see her there again. He never did.

Mitch did not see Joyce the rest of summer. He was right, it would be the only time he saw her at the pool. On the first day of school it was 99°. The pool closed for the season. "Why in the hell do they close the pool when it's still so hot?" his older sister said walking him to school. "I don't know," Mitch said as he realized summer was really over. But this wasn't just any summer. This was the summer when he bubble-kissed the most beautiful girl in school and nobody knew about it. He kept it a secret because he realized none of his friends or brothers would ever believe him and even if they did, Joyce might deny it. Joyce never told anyone either, but for different reasons. In her eyes, Mitch was a boy-toy for *one* summer day. She liked him more than she would ever admit to any of her friends, but it remained *their* secret.

IT WAS THE START of seventh-grade with a completely different set of peer-pressures and social connections. Joyce was now the prettiest girl in junior-high-school and still only twelve years old. Now, she had the pick of every boy in seventh, eighth *and* ninth grade. Mitch knew he could not compete with all those older, better-looking boys. But something was different about her. Whenever he would walk by and even when she talked with friends in the hallway she would smile and wave. She *never* did that before. Mitch would wave back, but not once did he walk up to her. It became an unspoken truth between them that what happened at the bottom of the pool on that hot August summer day would be *theirs* and theirs alone. The more he stayed away, the more she wanted him. But what could they do?

When Joyce found out Mitch was moving back home to Seattle she walked up to him one day in the hallway. It was the only time she ever did that. "I hear you're moving back to Seattle."

"Yeah, my dad just can't take the heat down here, says he can't breathe. It's kinda funny 'cause he's from Kentucky. He lived there a long time ago."

"Do you want to go back, Mitch?"

"No, I'm afraid to go back because I've made so many friends here. I really am scared, Joyce."

Joyce reached in her tiny white purse and pulled out a folded piece of blue-lined white paper and handed it to Mitch. "What's this?"

"It's my address. When you get back to Seattle will

you please write me and tell me how you're doing?"

"Sure, I mean if you really want me to."

She put her hand up to his right cheek and brushed it slowly with the back of her soft hand.

"Yes, I want you to write me. Promise me right now you will Mitch."

"I promise Joyce ... I promise." It was a promise Mitch could not keep.

WHEN HE RETURNED home to Seattle, everything had changed. A kid year is equivalent to about ten adult years. That meant Mitch aged almost twenty years. Funny, he did feel older.

A couple of months after he moved back, Mitch visited St. Luke's and the field of glory. It was strange; he stood there nearly two years to the day after the epic battle with Buster Crooks. It was dark and cold. Did the playground have memories? He stayed there a while and wondered if he would ever recapture the magic feeling he had just two years before.

Mitch had the uncanny ability of remembering things. Growing up, he was just naive enough to believe everyone could remember things. By the time he reached high school Mitch realized another super-power—his memory. He could tell you where he was and what he was doing on any given day. Not just what he was doing, what everyone around him was doing. From memory, Mitch could recall the smells, lighting, colors, temperature, his mood and the mood of almost anyone around him. He could walk into a crowded room and sense the feel. Big crowds made him nervous. Mitch didn't understand why. Too many things could go wrong in a big crowd. Maybe it was his need to absorb the mood of *everyone* around him—hard to do with thousands of people. So he just stayed away.

Well into his forties now, Mitch never married because he thought no woman could put up with his idiosyncrasies. That bothered him sometimes, but he didn't stay down long. *"The true measure of a man is how he picks himself up,"* his father once told him. Dad had so many great quotes and Mitch often wondered if he just made some of them up. He did, but would his son be the wiser? Mitch didn't care his dad stretched the truth—all he really knew is, he missed Dad and thought about him every day.

After a bad day he wished he could just pick-up the phone to hear Dad's voice. The words: "It'll be okay son" or "be careful out there," would always calm him down.

"Love you, Mitch."

"Love you too, Dad," was how each phone call ended. Those words no longer spoken, but never forgotten, helped Mitch through the tough and lonely times. Like his father, Mitch was proud of many things. "I love you, Dad," was top on the list—the last words spoken the last time he talked with his father. For Mitch that was enough. He would be all right.

TWO

THE RAIN LADY

IT WAS A COLD, BLUSTERY, WET FEBRUARY 29th MORNING when Mitch barged into the coffee shop. The red, digital, out-of-place, LCD clock read 9:12 AM. Two things were wrong: Mitch was there on a Sunday and it was *way* too early. The coffee shop just opened and the lone Barista was all smiles. Her name was Kayla, but Mitch didn't like the sound of that. A name given from baby-boomer parents that was supposed to be different. Kayla wanted to fit in. She liked the name, but was it her? Mitch took a syllable out and called her an affectionate "Kay" instead. He was the only one who called her that. It made her feel special. He made a select few coffee girls feel special. Kay was happy to see what she called her favorite customer. She had short bleach-blond hair to go with her small stature and a wide smile that exposed her straight white teeth. She carried a few extra pounds, but was easy on the eyes. Mitch always had a smile and something nice to say.

"Hey Mitch, whatta you doing here on a Sunday?"

Kayla worked weekends and Mitch *always* came in on Saturdays.

"Gettin' some coffee, got any here?"

"You're so funny, Mitch."

"And you're so cute." Mitch loved to flatter some girls. He waited for a shy smile followed by a little girl blush before ordering.

"What can I make for you?" Kay said still flattered by the compliment.

"How 'bout a double-tall-almond-mocha, *extra hot.*"

"Coming right up, sir," Kay said happy Mitch was there to talk to. Old enough to be her father, Mitch still understood the awkwardness of youth. An awkwardness for him that would not go away—he just grew accustomed to it. It was easier to talk to girls Kay's age. His middle-aged body acquiesced to the youthful enthusiasm of his mind. He understood Kay—the only difference, Mitch realized his teen-age ambitions were either dormant or dead. He wouldn't let Kay know that and greeted her lofty goals with a polite, "Go for it, baby."

Kayla still had that sweet innocent aura and Mitch would not do or say anything to tarnish that innocence. Besides, he did not want to be anyone's dream killer. She would have plenty of time to find out later.

"YA GONNA STAY AWHILE TODAY MITCH?!" Kay shouted over the high-pitched swishes of the espresso machine—milk steamed to one-hundred-seventy-degrees. Then she pulled the silver mug off the steamer and watched the thermometer slowly rotate clockwise to one-hundred-eighty. Precisely the temperature Mitch preferred. He waited until the espresso burps subsided and looked at her with a boyish smile and said, "Maybe." It was a rare day Mitch had all to himself. And he was unwilling to commit. Even to his *favorite* hangout.

If this was a Saturday, Mitch would stay until around 11:30 and then head to the pool for his customary lap swim between noon and one. He usually swam three times during the weekdays, but only an act of God could make him miss a Saturday swim. But this was a Sunday and the pool was closed. Sometimes he would run across someone he knew and then as his father before him, get lost in a story. No one seemed to mind. Mitch could tell a good story.

Mitch finished his coffee with the usual—"Mmmm that was good baby." Since no one else had entered while he was there it was one quick trip to the restroom, and then hit the road. The downside to his coffee habit—a lot of peeing. "Keeps my system clear," he would boast to his friends. *Excessive peeing* because he also drank a lot of water.

He bolted out the bathroom for a quick goodbye just as the front door burst open with the clash of wind and rain, followed by the dull, ringing, old worn-out bell, Mitch could not quite get used to. It was nasty out there—getting darker when it should have been lighter. Kayla said with a little girl pout, "Ya leaving so soon, Mitch." Before he could answer he saw a lonely-looking lady dressed in dark clothes. She stared right into his eyes—as if to say—*stay*. She was still in the doorway shaking off the rain from her black umbrella, when Mitch answered, "I believe I *will* stay awhile."

They avoided each other until the gravitational pull of curiosity drew them together. She sat on the old pale-green cloth couch next to his table, facing him. The old green couch did not fit in with the other decor yet people were drawn to it.

Mitch pretended to read the paper, but kept sneaking peeks at her over the top of the sports page. She shook the excess water from her shiny dark-green hooded raincoat and draped it over a chair. "There are twenty tables in this place and she picks this couch," Mitch muttered to himself in a low inaudible tone behind his paper. Instead of feeling flattered he was nervous. He started to sweat a little. She was right across from him reading a tiny paperback book with legs crossed and one leg swaying back and forth like a metronome. This highlighted black leather boots with just enough heels to get noticed.

She wore tight, dark-gray jeans that fit well in all the right places. Mitch paid particular attention to her long black hair and pale-white face. She had a smirk he didn't like. How could anyone look so comfortable— so cool? That's the thing, no one could be *that* calm. Mitch sensed her cool composure was a façade. He wanted to test his theory. Mitch looked at her a dozen times, but she was lost in the book. Not knowing what else to do, he put down the paper and said, "So tell me everything you know, I've got a minute to spare."

As soon as he said that, Mitch realized two things: One, this was the wrong thing to say, and two, he had seen this woman before. Something was different. As she opened her mouth and said, "Excuse me, are you talking to me sir?" Mitch realized the difference. Her hair was darker and she was without the cute blonde-haired, blue-eyed, little-boy. It tripped up Mitch a little and he was embarrassed by it. He always bragged he could recognize anyone, anywhere, even if he hadn't seen them for a long time. At a loss for words Mitch exacerbated the problem by answering: "Do you see anybody else in here?"

The darkly dressed lady uncrossed her legs, set up on the couch and said, "I see *you*." Here was a woman whose personality matched the clothes she wore. A mysterious, almost dark aura, exuded from her. She knew she made him nervous and was having a good time doing it. Mitch *was* nervous, but that wasn't going to stop him.

"Where's the cute little boy I've seen you with?"

"He's not my boy; he's my ex-boyfriend's kid." It

made sense because that kid looked nothing like this lady.

"So where is he?"

"Oh we broke up and he kicked me out of his house."

"Sorry to hear that—do you still see that kid?"

"No I don't and I really miss him."

"What about your ex, do you miss him too?"

"Sometimes, but it was a rocky relationship." Relaxing a bit, Mitch got up and came over to the couch. "Mind if I sit down" he asked politely. He was surprised when he noticed a slight blush and a soft, "No, I would like that." Was this a trap, or did she really want to share her story? He was determined to find out.

Mitch didn't know what compelled him to walk over and sit next to this stranger. She had *the look*. Somewhere in the cocky smile was a lost and lonesome lady. This was Mitch's unpredictable side. A mystery to the women he had known throughout his life. They would say, "You just never know what he's gonna do." Mitch couldn't explain some things he did. The thing that scared him the most was being called *normal*. Not a problem for Mitch—nobody *ever* called him normal.

THE ANNOYING RED clock switched from 9:59 to 10:00 AM as Mitch sat down beside his new friend. She wasn't really a friend, but he couldn't help his curiosity. He wanted to know more.

"I don't believe I introduced myself properly, my name's Mitch."

"Oh, nice to meet you, I'm Sarah." She made a feeble attempt to lift a hand in a gesture of kindness. It seemed she did not want him to touch her. He would have to stretch himself across the couch to reach her hand, which barely extended a few inches from her body. Not wanting to look like a dork, Mitch stood up and extended his hand right in front of her face. With this gesture there would be no confusion about his intentions.

"Nice to meet you, Sarah," he said looking down into her light-grey eyes. Sarah had no idea what to make of this intriguing stranger. Mitch had already made an indelible impression—going out of his way to make sure he could stand in front of her for a proper greeting. When he did, Sarah noticed something strange. His hand was the softest and warmest she had ever touched on a man. It bothered her. How could a man with such rugged exterior have such a soft hand? Sarah thought his hand should be *rough*— like his personality.

Mitch just waited to see the look in her eyes when he touched her. Her eyes widened and he pulled his hand away. He sensed an uneasy, almost cold glare.

"Is something wrong?" Mitch asked with a stern but cautious voice.

"No it's just your hand, I mean, it's so ..."

"So what?"

"Soft."

"Sorry to disappoint you," Mitch snapped. "These are the only hands I got."

"Can I ask what you do?" Sarah said sensing his hostility.

"Now why do you want to know that?"

"Just curious," knowing all the while she was actually anxious. She had presumed the ultimate indignity; basically calling him a wimp because of his soft extremity.

"I break rocks with my hands for a living!" Mitch blurted out proudly. Sarah started to giggle. Just a little at first. When it didn't stop for almost a minute, Mitch soon joined in until they both laughed so loud, Kayla looked over at them with a semi-jealous glare.

"We're okay Kay, just told her how much you love me, that's all."

"WHATEVER, MITCH!" Kayla shouted as she turned to serve a customer through the drive-up window. No one else had been inside the coffee shop yet. In the late-morning hours on a rainy Sunday, Sarah and Mitch were getting to know each other. She didn't know if he was trying to romance her, but did know, whatever he was doing, *she liked it.*

"So ya gonna tell me what you do?"

"You first," Mitch insisted.

"I work in real estate."

"For yourself?" Mitch asked as he noticed her body leaning over closer to him.

"I *wish*. I work for a big company that takes my profits."

"Funny how it works, you toil, they take." Mitch said.

"Yeah, I know, I'm waiting ..."

"Oh yeah, I'm a carpenter. How do you think I got these soft hands?"

Giggling some more Sarah said, "You really are funny, Mitch. Do you work for yourself or another company?"

"I work for myself. So the IRS takes away my profit. Lately though it's been tough."

"What you mean?"

"Nothing really, I have plenty of work. I should by now because I've been in business for almost twenty-three years. But lately I've had some doubts."

"What kind of doubts, Mitch?"

"Whether I chose the right career, or if I should've gone to college. I just can't see myself sitting behind a desk looking at a computer screen all day. That would drive me freaking nuts."

"You don't look like you belong behind a desk. You should be proud of what you do. You build things and create things. I think it's very commendable."

"It's also very *scary*. I don't think you have any idea what it's really like. It can be lonely, too. I remember when I started and did new construction. No one lived in the houses so I could work as late as I wanted. Some nights I would work until midnight and not get home until one in the morning. I would pass out watching TV and wake up in the morning with a half empty box of cold pizza."

"How many years did you do that?"

"More than I care to remember. I had no money and needed new equipment and a reliable truck. The only way to get those things was to work, *all the time*. It got to the point to where it didn't matter what day it was—just another day of work.

"I had no social life. I would go to get my hair cut and the girl who cut my hair would ask what I was doing that weekend. My response was always the same: 'Same thing I do every weekend, *work*.' She looked at me like I was some kind of *freak*. It's not that I wanted to work all the time, but since I started my business with nothing, I had no choice. I was just twenty-three years old and some people looked at my ambition like a disease."

"Sometimes I have to show houses on the weekends and evenings. I hate being in someone else's house with a stranger, especially at night. Believe me, Mitch; every job has its downfalls. I think you work too much, but it sounds like you like it. Do you?"

"Most of the time, and don't get me wrong, having too much work is better than *not* having enough and I've been there many times. It just gets lonely sometimes Sarah, especially when you have no one to go home to."

Sarah could see sadness in Mitch's eyes. She wanted to console and comfort him with profound phrases like: "don't worry, you'll find somebody" or "maybe you were meant to be alone," but realized he didn't need to hear it. No one needed to hear it. Although she could not understand *why* he was alone she completely understood he *was* alone.

Sarah looked down at Mitch's hands.

"Still wondering 'bout my hands?"

"Yes, it's puzzling."

"No mystery, I just wear those latex gloves—protects them and keeps 'em soft."

It still didn't explain the smooth, surgeon-like extremities Mitch possessed.

"Can I see your hands Mitch?"

"Sure, do anything you want with 'em."

Sarah grabbed his hands and put them both flat on her thighs, in front of her with the palms up. She circled her index finger around the palm of his left hand. She noticed a scar right at the joint of the middle finger.

"WOW, looks like something took a bite out of you here!"

"Just a saw blade," Mitch said a little embarrassed hoping she wouldn't prod further.

"Jeez, does it still hurt?"

"Only when I use it."

"How'd that happen?" Sarah said realizing Mitch didn't want to divulge the slip-up.

"Look, can we just move on ..."

"Oh God, I'm sorry, sometimes I don't know when to shut ..."

"Forget it."

Still uncomfortable with each other they both noticed a mood change. Mitch didn't want to spend the rest of the morning talking about a stupid blunder. Sarah had already made hers, prodding too deep too soon. Mitch wanted to leave and Sarah wanted to hide. Finally he broke the tension: "Mind if I ask what happened with you and your ex?"

"Ask me anything you want," she said glad they were talking again.

"Why did ya break-up?"

"We didn't break-up; I told you he kicked me out."

"Okay, why did he do that?"

"It's a long story and I don't think you would be interested."

Mitch smiled and moved a little closer, "I would be *very* interested."

"You know you can be charming when you want to."

"I bet you say that to *all* the boys."

"No, I don't."

Sarah wanted to talk somewhere more private even though Kayla was at least thirty feet away, book in one hand while twirling her hair with the other.

"We could go upstairs but I must warn you, there's not much room."

"Take me up there Mitch and I will tell you everything."

This is what Mitch wanted. What he yearned for, a stranger sharing her secrets. He had no way of knowing all the sorrow inside her. What he did know is from the first moment he laid eyes on her, the measure of the depth would be deceiving.

They ascended the wooden spiral staircase. Mitch led the way. She followed him up, staying close. Mitch already felt connected with this woman, but was afraid to say anything, for fear of it being one-way. When they reached the top and went through the door, Sarah could see the options: A tiny red plastic table (and white chairs) or the romantic wooden bench.

"Pick your poison," Mitch said hoping she would choose the bench.

"That table looks stupid, let's sit on the bench."

"Yeah I've always had a fantasy about *smashing* it with a sledgehammer."

"I'd love to see that. It doesn't belong up here."

They sat on the bench slightly tilted toward each other. If someone entered the room, he would notice from their almost touching knees, to their hips, resembled a giant V. They were close, *very close* but still not touching. Sarah put her left hand on Mitch's right knee and smiled.

"I'm glad you asked me up here; I've wanted to tell my story for a long time, but thought no one would understand."

With a puzzled look Mitch said, "Not even your girlfriends?"

"Especially my girlfriends, they would *never* get it."

"So why me, I mean, why tell me?"

"Don't ask me that again, Mitch, besides I think you know why."

Sarah must have sensed something in Mitch different from anyone else. She could feel it, his inner calm, yet total vulnerability. The rough exterior masked a well-hidden inner sensitivity. She had him pegged, or so she thought. Could she look right through him? This was the reason she made him nervous. A strange lady who came in from the rain, already knew Mitch better than most—but how?

The one thing Sarah could not know is how well Mitch paid attention to everything. How could anyone know? The other thing Sarah didn't realize, Mitch was revealing himself—not holding anything back. Give her the emotional tornado and see if she can handle it. He only did this to someone he liked and thought he could trust. For Mitch Lucas that was saying something. He never *completely* trusted anyone. Sarah was special. He didn't want to persuade Sarah into telling her story so he just waited . . . . It was her turn.

She turned her body all the way toward Mitch, put her feet under that round well-proportioned butt and looked him in the eyes. This elevated her slightly on the narrow bench. Mitch liked the slight angle in which she looked down on him. Mitch leaned his body as far as he could toward her. Again, Sarah grabbed both of his hands then moved her face well into his comfort zone and said, "I will not ask you to keep my story a secret because that would be asking you to make a promise you might not keep." Mitch tried to console her, but Sarah quickly put her index finger over her mouth.

"Don't Mitch, just *try* to listen to me right now, just please keep what I tell you to yourself until we no longer see each other. I know it sounds weird, but from the moment I first saw you I could tell you were different. I don't know why I trust you because I have such 'issues' with men in that area. I walk in here today and you just come right up to me and grab my hand and look me in the eyes the way you did. Why did you do that?"

Looking more like a confused boy than a confident man, Mitch simply said, "So it's okay for me to talk now?"

"Of course it is you brat."

"Just makin' sure—Sarah, to tell the truth; *I* don't understand some things I do. I don't understand *me*."

"Goddamn you, Mitch, I really hate your honesty."

"Hate, now *that's* a powerful word—never cared for the word. Try my best not to use it."

"Why does it bother you?"

"God help me, you really wanna know? Okay here's the list: I hate work, people, relationships, God, Satan, punk rock, the blues, my neighbors and even some of my friends." Poppin' up to his feet like a Jack-in-the-box, Mitch pulled Sarah up from the bench, stuck his face *way* in her space, and put his lips less than an inch from hers. With his still power-ful, bitter, coffee-breath he said, "How 'bout this baby, do you *hate this*?"

Mitch pulled away and sat down almost as fast as he got up. Sarah was at a loss for words. She had just experienced one of the most exciting moments with a man in her life and no sex was involved. Not even a *kiss*. All Mitch could say was, "So can we get to your story before you start hating me." Laughing, Sarah looked at Mitch and with a condescending tone said, "Has anyone ever told you you're strange?"

"Every damn day. Listen the line runs all the way around the block and you're standing in front." Sarah confirmed what Mitch had known since he was old enough to look in a mirror and understand that a stranger was looking back at him.

"Look, I know I'm different, but what about you? I mean it takes one to know one, right?"

"Fair enough, Mitch, I'll tread lightly from now on." Sarah sat back down and took a deep breath as Mitch tried to relax. Through the tiny rectangular window he could see leafless trees shutter in the cold late-February wind. But he was inside, with her, up in a room where young lovers go—warm and dry.

"My ex-boyfriend's name is Frank. We were set up by a mutual friend. He took me to a funny movie on our first date and we couldn't stop laughing. It was so easy to be around him in the beginning. The thing I loved in those early days is he would always call me and ask how I was doing. I miss that—I do. Sometimes I miss him but ..." Sarah's eyes began to well-up. Mitch sensed some apprehension and tried to calm her down, "Look Sarah, if this is too hard we can forget about it. I'd feel bad if I talked you into telling me something you aren't ready for."

"That's very considerate Mitch, but I am *so* ready to share this story. Just don't judge me or think less of me if I break-down and cry."

Looking a little insulted Mitch said, "Don't be silly, I would never do that, Sarah."

"Thanks, Mitch. Anyway we really hit it off. The little boy's name is Daniel and he became the son I never had. Frank worked graveyard shift and I spent a lot of time with Daniel—fixing him breakfast and getting him ready for school. The odd thing about him is after Frank left for work around eleven p.m. each work night, Danny, I would call him, would sneak into bed with me. 'I'm so glad you're here Sari,' he would call me, 'Daddy is so mean to me sometimes.' I suppose that was the first of many red flags."

Looking alert, yet anxious, Sarah focused on her story. It seemed to Mitch she was now re-living it. While talking she avoided eye contact. Would Frank come running up the stairs to scold her? Her uneasiness built up as the words came out.

"I walked Danny to the bus each morning at eight-thirty. Frank had a long commute home after work he always complained about. I don't know what time he got home because after I dropped Danny off at the bus I would just go straight to work. So I hardly ever saw him in the mornings, even on the weekends because I had to work. Danny said he was real mean in the morning. I found out later just how mean.

"I moved in with Frank in early September. Danny had just started the second grade. There were lots of kids at the bus barn every morning along with mothers who complained about their husbands and life in general. I loved Danny (still do) but I did not want to end up like them. Did *any* of these women enjoy their lives? I often wondered their husband's side of the story.

"I was worried because Danny and I soon became like a mother and child. Frank seemed okay, but I realized if anything happened between us I would miss Danny so much. The first day after spring break everything changed."

"What happened?" Mitch asked, knowing when a woman says 'change' in a relationship is usually means something bad.

"On the first Monday morning after spring break, I couldn't get Danny out of bed. He pushed and screamed and said he hated me, hated school and hated life. Something snapped in him and he shouted, 'I HATE GOD!'

"'Settle down Danny, we need to get ready for school.'

"'I HATE SCHOOL, I'M NEVER GOING BACK!'

"'You have to get ready for school Danny, NOW!'

"As we were wrestling to get him ready I saw a dark blue spot just above his underwear line. He settled down and I gently pulled down the back of his briefs. A deep-blue bruise from the small of his tiny back down almost to the crack of his butt stared back at me. I am *not* kidding, Mitch; this bruise was at least six inches long and almost as wide."

"Jesus, what did you do?" Mitch asked, sitting up in the bench.

"What could I do? I didn't know what to say. I think he knew I saw it because he was real quiet—we both were until he started sniffling, slowly at first, until emotions got the best of him. He exploded into loud crying as he grabbed my arm and wouldn't let go.

"'Don't ever leave me here alone Sari, *please*. Daddy is so mean sometimes, don't ever leave …'

"'It's okay, Danny, I won't. I promise I won't.'

"'I'm so scared all the time, Sari, please don't leave me. Say you won't leave, *promise* me!'

"'I promise, Danny, I promise.'

"'I love you, Sari, you're nice to me.'

"'I love you too, Danny, you're a good boy.'"

"My God, what did you do next?" Mitch said ready to crawl out of his skin.

"I held him in my arms and cried with him until he stopped. I knew I would always love him after that—kinda like a mother knows no matter how much her kid's screw-up, she will love them, unconditionally. He's such a cute boy with his blond hair and blue eyes."

"Yeah, I saw him here with you one time, looked like a young Robert Redford."

Giggling again Sarah asked Mitch when he had seen her.

"It was right before my birthday so it must have been in early July. I remember thinking that little kid looked so happy. It was a hot day and you were wearing shorts with a purple blouse; low cut to show-off your boobs."

"I wasn't trying to show-off my boobs."

"Sure looked that way to me, but it's okay, I mean if I had boobs like yours I would want to advertise them too."

Laughing she said, "I enjoy talking with you, Mitch, you make me laugh, but I'm wondering about you."

"Really, when you figure it out will you let me know?"

"Sure, but how did you remember the top I wore and shorts for that matter?"

"Have you seen yourself in shorts and a low-cut blouse? I notice things. Things most people don't. I like purple, especially the dark-purple you wore that day. And the kid, I mean how many times do you see a boy like him?"

"God, he *is* a cute kid." A sad look came over her face as if to say, 'I miss you Danny.'

"You don't remember me from that day, do you?" He asked hoping she would. "No, I don't Mitch, but not because of you."

"Right after that day we broke-up. We went on a camping trip to Lake Chelan for the 4th of July. We came back early the morning of the 5th. While driving back home, Danny was screaming and Frank kept yelling at him to shut-up or else … 'Shut-up or else what,' I muttered out loud. Right when I said it I knew it was a mistake, but it was too late. I could see a look on his face I hadn't seen before. I waited for his wrath.

"'What I say to my son is none of your damn business you bitch. It might be a good idea for you to sit there and keep your mouth shut.'

"'And if I don't?'

"'I'll have too …'

"'Hit me like you hit *him*—so hard it leaves a bruise for two weeks. My God Frank, he's just a little boy, how could you?'

"'I told you bitch, mind you own fucking business.'

"'Quit talking like that in front of him, you're scaring him, he told me he's scared all the time.'

"Suddenly he hit the brakes and we skidded off the road. He got out of the car and grabbed all my things in the trunk and tossed them in the brush. Then he opened the passenger door and said calmly this time, *'Get out.'*

"'I'm not getting out here; I don't even know where we are.' He grabbed my hair and said one more time as he pulled me out of the car. Only this time he wasn't so calm.

"'I'm not telling you again bitch, GET OUT!'

"Before I knew it, I was on the ground. It was hot and dusty and I had no idea where we were. The last thing I remember is being dragged by my hair and Danny screaming, 'NO DADDY, NO!' Then it was lights out. I woke up in the brush with my overnight bag and suitcase, but no cell phone. He probably smashed it. I don't think I was out very long because the back of my legs were still bleeding a little from when he dragged me into the brush. The back of my head hurt because I think he hit me or maybe I hit a rock when he dragged me. I don't know. It was a Sunday and still early. I don't remember seeing anyone on the road. I don't think anyone saw what happened. I wanted to find him and kill him, Mitch."

"You're lucky he didn't kill *you*, I think you're lucky to be sitting here telling me this story."

"I really don't need a lecture right now, Mitch." Sarah grew impatient.

"Sorry, I didn't mean to ..."

"I know, Mitch, it's just I can't believe I didn't see it coming. I feel so stupid."

"Quit blaming yourself. How could you know? You date someone for a while and you think you know them, but what do you *really* know about them? Then a few weeks or months go by and they lose their temper or get drunk. Then you're in their medicine cabinet one day and you see *way* too many pills." Mesmerized by Mitch's insight Sarah interrupted: "Do you look in your girlfriend's medicine cabinet?"

"I do now."

"Can I ask why?"

"Let's just say I got involved with the wrong girl—a meth addict and pill popper. And if I'm gonna get involved with anyone else I wanna know. It's a long story, probably longer than yours so I really don't want to go into it."

"Oh, Mitch, please tell me more—you've sparked my curiosity."

"Okay, but remember *you* asked. Look, the bottom line is: If you're a drug addict, especially a meth addict and I date you, I will find out. It's the only real thing I learned from dating and living with a drug addict for a year."

"Oh my God, a year! And you didn't know?"

"I didn't know anything about meth. In my day there was pot, booze, coke and acid. I know there were other drugs but pot and booze were the easy ones. I did my share of both."

"You took LSD?" Sarah said wondering why he mentioned it along with the others.

"I didn't say that," Mitch said realizing a hint of self-incrimination.

"That means you did, Mitch."

"Okay, if that's what you want to believe. The point is we knew what we were getting and more importantly, *who* we were getting it from. Now days they mix shit together and next thing you know you got crack or meth—something that gets you hooked the *first* time you try it. Do you know what they cut some meth with?"

"Jesus, Mitch, I really don't, look I can see you're upset so we can drop ..."

"*Drano*, no kidding and you know what, it works."

Sarah was hooked now, she *had* to hear this.

"What does Drano do, why do they use it?"

"I don't know *why* they use it, probably just to add shit to more shit but I can tell you what it does ...

"Right after she moved in with me I noticed the water in my tub filling up whenever I took a shower. No big deal, I'd put some Drano in it and everything was fine. But it kept happening."

"What kept happening?"

"The drain in the bath tub silly, it kept getting clogged. So one day after she went to work I took off the cover and saw blond hair. I must have pulled the amount you see on a Barbie doll. And she had only been living with me two weeks. It didn't make sense. How could someone only twenty-four lose so much hair?"

"My Mitch, I see you like em *young*."

"Not after her, too much work and drama."

Mitch was upset. Every time he brought up this girl, a messed up meth addict, he got irate. He talked when he should've listened. "How the hell did we get on this subject?" Mitch asked Sarah. "First, you finish, Mitch; I gotta know what happened with this blond chick."

"Okay, but it gets pretty ugly and don't say I didn't warn ya."

"I'm thirty-four *not* twenty-four, I can handle it."

Mitch stood up and started to pace the floor. He looked out the window again. He was tense, wondering what Sarah would think of him for being involved with a loser, drug addict and drama queen. He stood over by the narrow window leaning with one arm on the ledge. His body was slightly tilted toward the wall and the other arm inverted with one hand on his hip. A classic stance he inherited from his father— executed unknowingly and perpetuated with pride.

Mitch looked down at the tops of huge photinias as the wind pushed the shiny red and green sides of some leaves to their dull grey backside color. "It's windy out there, Sarah, February is one of the bleakest months."

"I don't care about the wind right now, Mitch, I'm worried about you. All of a sudden you look sad. Can I ask why?"

"You can ask, but I don't think I will *ever* be able to express the effect she had on me. I mean the strangeness of it all. The drugs, the drama, the ending, it all seems like a dream now."

"Did you love her, Mitch?" Somehow he knew she would ask.

"I think you know the answer Sarah. I'm ashamed of it now, but at one time I loved her more than anything in this world."

"Why are you ashamed? I mean once you love someone it should be forever, right?"

Mitch walked back over to the bench, sat down, tilted his head back about six inches from the wall and took a deep breath. "Where did you hear that bullshit, Sarah, some little-girl fairy tale? Let me share a secret with you, *nothing* lasts forever."

"You sound so final."

"When love ends, it is final."

"I did love her, but I've lost all respect. And when the respect goes, so does the love. Don't ever forget that Sarah. I was stupid, I admit it. She would ask me for money to buy groceries when I knew she would spend it on meth or booze. The whole time this was happening I was becoming a different person. Drinking more and smoking pot with her. I pretended things were normal. The most horrifying thing in all this was the crash and burn effect."

"I almost hate to ask, Mitch, but what does that mean?"

"Well you see she would go visit her sister in Spokane and be gone for about a week. This was fine with me because I didn't want her around anyway. When she got back her lips were almost as white as her face. Becoming honest she would admit she had been up for five days and nights doing meth. From ten feet away I could feel the meth oozing out of every pore. Like some evil invisible lava moving down a mountain to rebuild itself. Her meth habit could never be extinguished. The addiction *had* to be fed.

"Every time she came down from that drug she was a walking time bomb. I would almost prefer to have her 'strung out' all the time than to invoke her wrath while coming down. The problem with meth users is almost all of them stay addicted for life."

"Jeez, poor thing I wonder how she got so messed up?" Sarah said sadly.

"Yeah, poor Frank, I wonder how he got so messed up?" Mitch said sarcastically.

Sarah returned a look Mitch had seen from other women many times before. Did she understand the ramifications of that statement? There was another moment of silence between them. Mitch hoped Sarah would carefully contemplate a response. He liked her and did not want to lose a friendship yet to develop. But Mitch was a realist and understood what could happen. *Any* friendship can be destroyed in an instant.

"Look, Sarah, I knew you would defend her, every woman has, all her life. What they do not realize is they are actually *enabling* and perpetuating her drug habit."

"Hey, you never told me her name or how you met."

"Her name doesn't matter now; she's dead as far as I'm concerned."

"I don't think it's fair to compare my ex to yours Mitch."

"Oh I know, because he's a man, and when a man is a drug addict or meth user things are easy, he's a *loser,* pure and simple. But when I tell you my young blond ex-girlfriend did the same thing, she's a *victim.* It's okay; I've heard it all before, but *never* from a man. I'm sure Frank was a decent guy at one time, but something happened or he came from a family of alcoholism and from what you tell me he probably was abused as a child."

"He was. Look Mitch I see your point, it's one of those things society labels men as. I know it's wrong.

I wasn't saying *poor thing* as an excuse for her to shit all over you. I was just saying poor thing as in she must have had something horrible happen to make her ..."

"MAKE HER LIKE THAT!" Mitch interrupted loudly. "Yeah every drug addict has some lame excuse to make them like that. Make them steal, lie and fuck other people behind your back. Make them break all the things you love and cherish. Oh yeah, it's never any of their shit because they *need* that to *sell* for more drugs. Make them go crazy and scratch you down your back so hard there's rolls of your flesh under their fingernails. Make them bite, kick, scream and pull your hair so hard it hurts for days. Make them ..."

"My God, she really did all those things to you? Okay, Mitch, okay, I know the answer."

"DO YOU?! I warned you it wasn't pretty. When drugs and alcohol and especially meth, wield their ugly side no one wants to stick around and clean-up the mess. And it does get messy, believe me."

"I do Mitch, I really do. I'm sorry it sounded like I was on her side, but I have to know one thing, how did you get involved with her?"

"I was alone and so was she. She worked at the grocery store bakery close to my house. I would walk there and I'd see her almost every day, but didn't say anything."

"How long did that go on, I mean before you did anything?"

Mitch pulled out some gum neatly packed in a tablet dispenser and popped one in his mouth.

"Want one, Sarah?"

"Sure, Mitch thanks."

Calming down, he pulled his right leg up and let it rest on his left leg so the right ankle bone rested just above his knee. He grabbed the right leg with both hands on his shin and gave it a gentle tug while rocking his body back and forth.

"It's hard you know, looking back, knowing the moment you made that big mistake."

"What mistake, Mitch?"

"For me it was asking her out. I hate asking a girl out. Not just her, *any* girl. But I picked her. I call it the Jack Chesbro effect."

"*What*, I mean, *who* the hell is Jack Chesbro?" Sarah said obviously baffled.

"He was a pitcher for the New York Highlanders a long time ago. You probably never heard of them, but they later became a team we Seattleites love to hate: the New York Yankees. I suppose we hate em' because they know how to win and we don't. Anyway, Mr. Chesbro was having his best year on the mound in 1904. He won 41 games. Almost *half* the team's total for the year. And he only lost 12. *Any* pitcher who wins 41 games in a season is superhuman. In fact, no pitcher has done it since. Over a *hundred years*. And let's face it, the way these candy-ass Prima Donnas complain about the slightest injury these days, it's safe to say Mr. Chesbro's record is untouchable. He also started 51 games that year and completed an unbelievable 48 of them. His arm must've been made from iron."

"Okay, Mitch, I get it, the baseball players back then were tougher; everybody was. But what does this have to do with your ex-girlfriend?"

"It has *everything* to do with her if you'll let me finish."

"Sorry, Mitch, go ahead."

"On the final day of the season in 1904, the New York Highlanders were a game and a half behind their rivals, the Boston Americans. They were playing a doubleheader at home and needed both wins to secure the American League pennant. Jack Chesbro pitched the first and what turned out to be most memorable game of the season. It was the top of the ninth inning in a 2-2 battle when his spitball sailed over the catcher's head. Boston had a man on third base and *the wild pitch* allowed the winning run to score. New York failed to score in the bottom of the ninth so Boston won the pennant. No one cares they couldn't come up with a run when they needed it, or won the second game, but *still* lost the pennant. All anyone remembers is that *one* wild pitch: The spitball that got away."

"Sorry Mitch, but what is a spitball."

"That's right, you've probably never heard of it either. The spitball was used a lot back then. Some pitchers *still* use it, but will never admit it because they made it illegal a long time ago."

"Did they really spit on the ball?" Sarah said puzzled. "Some of them did, but all you need is a little moisture and the ball becomes unpredictable. So *unpredictable* it can fly over your catcher's head and cause you nothing but grief and heartache the rest of your life. If Mr. Chesbro were here today I'm sure he would tell you: 'I wish I could have that pitch back.'"

"So what happened to him?" Sarah said with a sudden interest in baseball, a sport she did not watch or even care for. That is, until Mitch changed baseball into something metaphoric, *life*.

"He pitched a few more years—even won over 20 games one year. But he was *never* the same. He never pitched in the World Series. He was eventually enshrined into the Hall of Fame in 1946, but that was fifteen years after he died."

"Good lord, what a depressing story."

"Not really, at least not the way I see it."

"Really, Mitch, tell me how can you take anything good out of that story?"

"Well my dear, how many people do you know have made it to the major leagues? I only know *one* and he is a friend of the family. Anyway, the point is, pitching at that level is hard. And winning 41 games at that level is *crazy*. But Mr. Chesbro did it. Sure, he had one bad pitch that cost him more than he could ever know. Don't we all do that? Don't we make that *one* bad pitch like I did in asking that drug addict out? Besides, Jack Chesbro's story is a love story."

This captured Sarah's attention more than anything else Mitch said that morning.

"What love story?"

"After Jack died in 1931 his widow spent the rest of her life trying to get the ruling changed on the call from a wild pitch to a passed ball."

"I don't understand, what would that do, I mean what would be the difference?"

"So glad you asked my dear. I won't explain the technical difference except to say Jack Chesbro was a lucky man. His wife defended his honor long after he died and that is, what you call, *true* love."

"I still don't understand."

"Let's just say, *true love* is rare. The bad pitch for me is when I asked her out. The pitch *I'll* never get back."

"Do you ask many girls to go out with you?"

"No, see that's the thing, I never got the hang of it I suppose, but I asked her. Not in the beginning because of the age difference. I didn't realize she could be interested in an old man like me. Nor could I realize how much she would take from me."

"What did she take from you?"

Sarah could not look Mitch in the eye when she asked this question. She could tell this girl, this meth addict, had a profound effect in every facet of Mitch's life. She just wanted Mitch to say it.

"She took my heart and I don't know if I will ever get it back. Even though I don't love her anymore, my heart is gone."

"I've never heard a man talk this way before. I'm so sorry, Mitch, really I am."

"Don't be, it's my fault."

"Then maybe you should just forgive her, not for her, I don't care about her, but it might be easier for you, Mitch."

"I'll try Sarah, but sometimes it's hard."

"Yes Mitch, it is. So how long did you wait to ask her out?"

"It was around two months. We finally started talking. She would make fun of my shorts and the way I walked. I loved the way she braided her long blond hair. When she turned around it would bounce around and rest just above her butt. She looked so young, so full of life and energy. I looked at her and saw me in the past. So when I did ask her out, I knew she would be trouble."

"What did she say; I mean what did *you* say to persuade her to go out with you?"

"Is that what you think, I have to *persuade* girls to get them to go out with me?"

"No, Mitch I don't and I believe you don't ask many out. There's just something about you that's strange. It's hard for me to describe, but I feel it. Other girls must feel it too ..."

"Feel what?" Mitch said a little discouraged.

"Your aura, it's hard to get around it. I hope you don't get pissed-off Mitch, but I think you make a lot of girls nervous. You make me nervous."

"Then why come up here with me and tell me

these secrets?"

"That's what scares me, I don't know why."

"Well, if it makes you feel any better, you make me nervous too, Sarah."

MITCH AND SARAH remained silent a few minutes. The awkwardness now was overwhelming. He was amazed at Sarah's insightful, yet bold analogy. She was right *and* wrong. He did not appreciate being categorized into one singular theory. Mitch was a little more complex. He stood up and started to pace again. He ended up over by the window again and noticed a low cloud cover moving fast. Clouds started to break apart. Mitch could see a pale silhouetted sun penetrate gray and white clouds. It looked like a giant transparent curtain. It was a brief break between rainstorms moving through that day in a winter Northwest sky. Again, Mitch was sure he was the *only* one to notice it. Sarah remained on the bench, oblivious, and did not move.

"Look Sarah, I don't want to scare you. I don't want to scare anyone. I know I'm strange, I've known it since I was a kid. My dad always told me, 'Don't follow the crowd son.' That's what I've tried to do my entire life. Maybe you see something in me a lot like you, maybe it scares *you*."

"Yes it does scare me but I know one thing for sure Mitch. I have never met anyone like you."

"I'll take that as a compliment."

"How did it end, Mitch, between you and the psycho?"

"Okay I'll tell you. Then you have to finish your story."

"It ended the way she said it would. She told me: 'The only way I'm ever leaving here is in handcuffs.' Sometimes drug addicts can be very insightful because that's precisely the way she left." Sarah looked puzzled. "You mean the cops just came and arrested her?"

"No, the cops just came and arrested her after she bit, scratched and clawed me like a bobcat. It's comical looking back on it now, but who was I to stop her prophecy? Somehow, in between the biting and scratching I managed to call 911. But I chickened out and hung-up the phone. The operator immediately called back so I grabbed the phone and went into the other room. My psycho-ex was in the bedroom yelling obscenities at me and the operator. She used just about every swear-word known and kept repeating loudly: 'YOU TELL THAT FUCKING BITCH I'M OKAY!' In a soft whisper I asked the 911 operator: 'Are you hearing this?'

"She must have sensed the gravity of the situation and said, 'I can hear every word and I'm going to send extra patrols to your house right away.'

"Three cops showed up at my house that night. One, an old veteran, had been there twice before and told her not to come back. He took her into our bedroom and the other two took me into my den. I saw one of them was young. He admitted it was only his second time out and both times were for domestic disputes. The other cop was around my age and got right to the point. 'What happened here tonight, Mitch?' I did not say a word. I just turned around while I took off my sweater to expose the scratches and perfect handprint on my back. The young cop said, 'DAMN, your back is covered with scratches and blood!' I said, 'It hurts.' They wanted to know if I had been drinking. I know how much cops *hate* when you lie so I told them I had three beers, which was the truth."

Sarah looked confused and asked. "Is that how it ended, I mean, what was the other cop doing with her in your bedroom?"

"They sure as hell weren't having sex, if that's what you mean."

Sarah giggled and told Mitch it was good he could joke about what happened. She did not anticipate a man like him exposing secrets in such a vulnerable way. Mitch was surprised too. Why did he reveal so much to this lady who came into the coffee shop out of the rain? It was too late now. Mitch was caught up in the moment and had to finish.

"So tell me Mitch, what was going on in your bedroom?"

"That's the strangest part of the story. The cop around my age told me to put my sweater back on and to see a doctor as soon as I could. They escorted me out the den and into my kitchen. As we walked into the kitchen, we passed my bedroom where the veteran cop was questioning the psycho."

"ALMOST TWO MONTHS before this happened she was on another nosedive off meth. In her usual meth withdrawal temper-tantrum she exploded into a violent rage and tore down both bedroom doors. And, of course, I was the one who had to fix them. When I propped them back up one was a little off center and there was about a one-inch-gap between them. I didn't take the time to fix them properly because I figured she would just rip them back down. Anyway, when I walked by my bedroom I could see and hear them talking. The old cop said, 'Have you been drinking tonight?' 'No, officer I haven't had anything to drink.' *Another* blatant lie.

"The gruff veteran cop barged out the bedroom doors like walking out of a saloon and said, 'Well she's going to jail.' The young rookie said, 'Hey, look at his back you gotta see it!' I just turned around and lifted my sweater and the old cop said, 'My, you better get that looked at son.' The psycho started to get unruly."

"Jesus Christ what a stupid bitch, didn't she realize what was happening?" Sarah said.

"Hey, it was just another meth-induced night to her. Relax Sarah it gets better. They told her to settle down or it was the body cuff. That got her attention and she quietly walked out the front door in handcuffs, her destiny fulfilled."

"My God, Mitch, I'm surprised you didn't hit her back."

"That's what the cop my age said when he questioned me after the young rookie and old veteran hauled her away. I told him I didn't want to hurt her. I mean what would that do? He told me I showed remarkable restraint and to remember everyone has the right to defend themselves. He took about twenty pictures of my back and noted I had a perfect red handprint of her hand on the middle of my back. All of this was logged as evidence but I didn't press charges."

"So that's it, did you ever see her again?" Sarah asked looking almost disappointed.

"Off and on for a while until my dad died. Then she was out of my life forever. The last time I talked with him was on Father's Day ten days before he died. Well, he brought up my ex-girlfriend and told me to stay away from her until she grew up. My dad had to *die* for me to realize he was right. Isn't that the most pathetic thing you have ever heard of?"

"Don't be so hard on yourself Mitch; I'm sure your dad understood what you were going through."

"He had *no* idea what I was going through. I'm glad I never told him the shit she did to me. He knew she was putting me through hell, but I did not tell him about the meth problem. I was already ashamed for being involved with such a loser. I felt like a *loser*. I didn't want my father to spend his last days on earth worried about me. He didn't deserve that."

"What about your mother, how did she feel about your young girlfriend?"

"She asked me why I was involved with a child. My mother did not like her from the beginning. I feel I let Mom down more than anyone."

"See, Mitch, that's the difference between you and your ex."

"Really, what difference?"

"You have a conscience and she doesn't. You care about people and I can tell how much you love your parents. You speak as though your father is still here. I can tell how much you miss him, Mitch. I'm sorry for your loss." Mitch looked away. Sarah knew she had struck a chord.

"I miss him every day, Sarah. It's not the same without him around. He knew the right thing to say. It wasn't always what I wanted to hear, but that never stopped him. Sometimes I wish I could pick up the phone and hear him say ..."

"It's okay, son, it's *okay*."

"Thanks, Sarah, for listening. Well, that was more than I thought I would divulge to *any* stranger. Can you finish your story? So you put on your sexy shorts so you could get a ride?"

"Whatever, Mitch, they were the only clean shorts I had and it was already hot outside."

Mitch felt guilty, but relieved for sharing his story. He had rambled on too long. He stood up, arms extended and leaned to one side with a tight-fisted stretch. Then he sat back down and looked Sarah right in the eyes. She looked worried.

"So what did you do next, hitchhike back? Hey you never told me, where the hell were you?"

"Somewhere around Lake Chelan, that's where we went camping the 4th of July weekend."

Mitch could tell Sarah was reliving the story again and was worried she would have some sort of anxiety attack. "Look, Sarah you don't have to go on, I mean if it's too hard for you, we could drop it." Sadness, all her own, was on Sarah's face. Crying, she reached for her purse and pulled out a vanilla colored handkerchief. "Hey, that's a cool snot rag." Sniffling and crying at the same time Sarah grabbed Mitch's hand and thanked him for listening.

"Can I finish, Mitch?"

"Yeah yeah, go ahead; I just hate to see you cry, doesn't sound like this bum is *worth* crying for."

"He's not, but I do anyway.

"Eventually, I got a ride from some old man in an old lime-green flatbed Ford pickup. He was a real gentleman and offered to take me anywhere I wanted to go. He wore light-brown overalls with an old floppy black hat. Looked like an old cowboy, just a little uncomfortable in his own skin. He didn't ask me what happened, just where I wanted to go as he looked straight ahead—hands so tight around the stirring wheel his knuckles were white.

"He didn't have a cell phone so I had him give me a ride back to Lake Chelan. I told him I had no money and the sweet old man gave me twenty dollars for the pay phone and breakfast. He even offered to drive me all the way back to Seattle. I told him no and thanked him for his kindness."

"Sounds like a real nice guy." Mitch said glad Sarah got a ride. "Probably an old farmer, I mean with no cell phone and the old flat-bed pickup."

"I guess you could call him a farmer. He said he owned a vineyard with five hundred acres of land. It was in his family for over a hundred years and he had no intention of ever selling it."

"You got lucky, Sarah, guys like that are a dying breed."

"I know Mitch; it was the only lucky break I got that weekend."

For the first time since they went up to 'the lovers' bench, *Sarah* stood up and walked over to the window. Looking out at the grey horizon she said, "I just hate winters around here, Mitch."

"Really, where you from?"

"Minnesota, it's cold there, but it doesn't rain like this, I mean every day."

"Not *every* day, it just seems that way. Minnesota is too freaking cold."

"Yes, it is cold, but not as wet, or dark. Seattle is so dark in the winter."

"Yeah, I love it. I've always preferred the dark. I love to take a walk in it and let it soak up my sorrow."

"You are *so* weird, Mitch."

"I know, finish your story?"

"Okay, Mitch, but I meant you're weird in a *good*

way. I had a friend come and pick me up. I did her a favor a long time ago and she owed me big-time."

"She drove *all* the way out to Lake Chelan from Seattle—man that's some friend."

"I know, Mitch, but she owed me. When she saw me she got all freaked out and wanted to call the cops. I told her to settle down and drive me back to his place. He lives in Edmonds and I had to see if Daniel was okay."

"Did you *want* another beating?"

"That's the weird part, Mitch, I wasn't afraid anymore. I wanted to see Danny so bad. When we got there I noticed some of my stuff outside. As we got closer I saw *all* my stuff—every single item I had in his house was outside lined up from the biggest items in back to the smallest in the front. It looked like a garage sale it was so organized."

"You sure know how to pick 'em."

"So do you Mitch."

"You got me there."

Sarah walked back over to the bench and sat down. They were now in their original position, except this time their knees were touching and Sarah grabbed both of Mitch's hands and held them tightly. "Please stay here with me, Mitch, until I finish."

"I told you I would. So what happened next?"

"I had my friend wait in the car across the street with her cell phone in case anything bad happened. I told her as soon as he started yelling to call the police. As I walked across the street, I saw the front door open and Frank come out. There was a lot of traffic and he was mumbling something, but I couldn't hear over the noise. My girlfriend thought he was yelling at me and called the cops. I looked back, saw her on the phone and knew there would be trouble."

"How long did it take for the cops to get there?" Mitch asked.

"About two minutes and then they were all over me. Apparently Frank called the cops when he saw my friend's car across street and *me* inside. He told the 911 operator I was stalking him and we had broken up over a week ago."

"How do you know that?"

"One of the cops told me. Frank's a fucking liar."

"He told me to get my stuff off the lawn. Then, he told *them* he hadn't seen me since we broke up."

"Damn, he is a liar. Did you tell them about the trip and what he did to you?"

"I did, but they didn't seem to care and I just wanted to get Danny out of the house. One cop was being rude and the other nice. The rude one acted like I was the troublemaker. Anyway I got lucky, the nice cop took me aside and I told him the entire story. He was very understanding, but told me there was nothing he could do. My stuff was on his property and I *had* to remove it. I kept asking him, 'What about Daniel?'

"'Unfortunately Miss, there is nothing I can do. You could call CPS and maybe they will look into it.

For right now, it's your word against his. Since it is his property we are required by law to remain present until you have removed all of your personal items. And you need to remove them and *yourself* right now.'"

"Jesus Christ, our hard earned tax dollars at work. Sounds like a couple of apathetic doughnut eating bums. Did you explain what happened over by Lake Chelan and how he knocked you unconscious? For God's sake, he could have killed you."

"I told him everything Mitch. But it happened in another county and he told me I would have to go to the local authorities and press charges. I asked them if I could have my girlfriend help me load my stuff into her car. The rude cop said okay, but to hurry up. God, he was an asshole. As we loaded her car, Danny came running out of the house crying and screaming: 'PLEASE DON'T GO SARI! PLEASE!' He ran up to me and latched onto my leg and wouldn't let go. The asshole cop shouted, 'LET THE BOY GO LADY, NOW!'"

Mitch could barely control himself as he got up and said: "I just *hate* cops who abuse their authority and have power trips over the people they're supposed to be serving."

"Settle down Mitch. The nice cop told *asshole cop* to leave me alone. Danny was crying and couldn't stop. He would not let go of my leg. Frank started yelling and told the cops to get me away from his son and the hell off his property. I guess the rude cop didn't like being yelled at and told Frank to go inside until they finished."

"Sounds like karma biting them both in the ass."

"Yeah, Mitch, I know. The rude cop didn't say much to me after that. I think he could sense Frank's evil side and realized I told the truth."

"Or he needed to get to the doughnut shop to meet his girlfriend."

Laughing some more Sarah said, "I can see you don't like cops, Mitch."

"No, I didn't say that, I just don't care for incompetent ones who mistreat people. And there's the cynical side of me that questions authority from anyone and everyone."

"Yes I can see, but hasn't it served you well in your life?"

"Yes and no. I just feel there's too much mindless conformity out there. I mean you're walking down the street minding your own business and out of nowhere a cop comes up to you and says: 'Can I see some identification?' Next thing you know you're emptying out your pockets. Then you're taking a ride in the back seat of the car. The only back seat where *no man* wants to be: *a cop car*. All this happened because you did not have the guts to stand up for your rights.

"I have great respect for *most* police officers. I feel they're doing their best in very difficult situations. The problem I have is some cops *should not* be cops. They know who they are and so does everyone around them. But no one will say shit. Not their partners, superiors or even their wives. Not until it's too late and they shoot some scared ten-year-old kid in the back because he didn't halt when he was supposed to. They don't follow procedure. They harass hardworking innocent citizens. And you know what? They like it—that is, until they run into somebody like me. Then I make it clear to them."

"What's that, Mitch?"

"Don't fuck with me unless you have a good reason."

"Good God Mitch, you remind me of that asshole cop."

"Ya see why I'm not a cop."

Sarah and Mitch shared their last good laugh together. In less than an hour they had revealed to each other more than they'd thought possible. This brought them together, but at the same time divided them immeasurably. There would be no romance between them. Too many secrets revealed too quickly and now the presence of each other's company had that familiar, yet uncomfortable feeling.

The sad look on their faces showed how the other felt. Mitch was perfectly aware and wanted Sarah to know he understood. But what could he say? He had already spoken too much. Sarah, if only for a moment, felt the same. There was another minute of silence before Mitch asked, "I almost forgot to ask you, Sarah, what about Daniel? Did you ever see him again?"

"No, Mitch, I never did after that day. I did call CPS and told them the whole story. They told me they would look into it. I don't know if they ever did. I hope they did, I really do. I keep thinking I will see Frank in the news sometime with a picture of Danny."

"Don't think like that Sarah, you did all you could. You should be proud. You probably showed Danny more love in the short time you knew him than *anyone* else."

Sarah cried again, then stood up with Mitch and hugged him. Mitch held her until the crying subsided. She said it was time to go. She wrote down her phone number and told Mitch he could call anytime he wanted. Mitch never did. Sarah understood why.

"I will not forget this day, Mitch, you're a special man."

"Oh yeah, well, you're better looking."

Sarah hurried down the spiral staircase saying how funny Mitch was. Mitch heard the door open and the bells dull ding. He couldn't help, but walk over to the window and look down. He saw a black umbrella pop up as the rain poured down. It was Sarah, leaving the way she arrived, in the rain*, the rain lady.* He thought about Mom and how he should be with her today. Mitch visited her every Sunday, it was their time together. But she had a cold and didn't want to make her son sick. So he came to the coffee shop instead. He missed Mom *and* Dad. He wondered what just happened and how he had changed. Sarah changed him. He already missed her. Mitch waited in silence until the sudden push of the front door exposed the faint sound of wind and rain. The bell rang louder than normal and Mitch wondered why. He hurried down the stairs.

THREE

DARK ANNIVERSARY

HEN MITCH GOT TO THE BOTTOM OF THE STAIRS the coffee shop was alive. Strange, he hadn't heard anyone come in except for the last customer. Sarah put him in a trance. The red LCD clock read 11:47 AM—brunch *or* lunch time. Take your pick. He looked around the room and saw almost every table was taken. The coffee shop served a few breakfast items, but Mitch didn't like any of them. Not much there was fresh and he is a picky eater. Kayla was relieved. Her help had arrived, a new girl Mitch hadn't seen before.

"Christy, I'd like you meet Mitch, my fav all-time customer." Kay said smiling.

"Oh yeah, Mitch, Kayla talks a lot about you."

Before he could respond it took Mitch about thirty seconds to take in all that was Christy. She was tall, at least 5'10" and skinny—a little too skinny, Mitch thought. She had jagged white teeth that revealed a self-conscience smile. Her long, dark-red hair was neatly braded into a pony-tail extending through the back of her black hat and almost down to her small butt. Mitch could see eyes that were green like his. Christy glowed of youthful exuberance.

"YA WANNA ANOTHER COFFEE MITCH?!" Kay shouted while *grinding* fresh espresso beans. Mitch moved in closer so he could smell the pungent aroma. Even as a kid he loved the smell of coffee. When he first tried it he quickly spat out what he called 'shit.' "Jesus Christ how does anyone drink this crap?" was his first reaction. Like so many other things in life, Mitch realized coffee was an acquired taste.

Christy walked to Mitch and asked, "Did you hear Kayla; she wants to know if you want another coffee?"

"I don't know, Whatta you think, should I?" Mitch asked.

Christy put her hand over her mouth to hide a smile as she looked and wondered about the man in front of her. It was the way Mitch looked at her—right *through* that made her nervous. Maybe it was just Mitch and the affect he had on some people. Kay warned Christy he would take time to warm up to. Kay said, "Just be careful what you say to him, he remembers everything." Christy could feel Mitch's eyes watching. She thought he was judging, "I bet he thinks I'm just another dumb barista." To Mitch, Christy looked confused. "Poor kid, she's new on the job. I'm gonna do something to make her feel better."

Mitch asked Christy if she would make him his favorite coffee. "Sure, Mitch, but are you sure you want me to make it?"

"Of course I'm sure, are you sure you can handle it?"

Christy, still uncomfortable, but now she wanted to show him what she could do. "So whatta have Mitch?"

"I'll have a double-tall, almond-joy-mocha, extra hot with 2% milk and a touch of whip. And don't scorch it. I want it extra hot, but not scorched." Now, Christy was really nervous. By the nature of the order, she could tell Mitch was picky about coffee. "I'm gonna go grab a table; please bring it over when it's ready."

"That'll be four dollars Mitch," Christie said proud of the exorbitant total. "FOUR BUCKS! It better be good for that much." Then he pointed at Christy and said, "You just make *sure* it's good."

Mitch went to the nearest available table and scrambled through what was left of the Sunday paper. Page after page of advertisements greeted him. He managed to find the obituary section and sat down to say goodbye to people he hadn't met. He was fascinated by their stories, their faces, and their accomplishments. Mitch wondered what would be written about him after he died. He believed he made a difference in this world, but was it enough to be remembered? Mitch looked at each face and hoped for answers.

Christy came with the coffee. "Here's your coffee sir, I hope you like it."

Mitch picked up the coffee and cradled it in his hands as he moved it from side to side just below his nostrils. "Smells good." Christy patiently waited for him to take a sip—worried her best effort wasn't good enough. "Please tell me how it tastes Mitch, and be honest; I want to know the truth."

Mitch raised the cup and sipped slowly not wanting to burn his mouth. He'd made that mistake many times with hot coffee and wasn't going to do it again, especially with this new young barista staring. When he removed his mouth from the hole atop the plastic lid he looked up at Christy. "That's the best damn coffee I've ever had." Mitch had just become Christie's favorite customer.

"Thanks Mitch, I'm glad you like it."

"Don't let it go to your head young lady. If you ever make me a bad coffee, you'll be the first to know."

"Okay Mitch, I believe you."

Mitch sat back in his chair and took a long slow look around the coffee shop. Every person at each table was engaged in conversation. Hand gestures with facial expressions to emphasize key elements of story. How could people be so engrossed in their own narrative and yet oblivious to their surroundings? He looked around at the nameless faces and recognized someone sitting at a booth away from the crowd—in the darkest corner. No paper, no coffee, just sitting there looking out the window. Mitch tried to remember the last time he saw this man and his name. That was Mitch's kryptonite; he was terrible with names. But he *never* forgot a face. He grabbed his coffee and walked over.

Mitch was about ten feet from the table when the man looked over and said, "Hey, Mitch, how ya doing?" Mitch did a quick-step and greeted him as he stood up. They exchanged a firm handshake, exemplifying two men who used their hands *and* their brains to make a living. "I'm sorry, I don't remember your name, I remember just about everything else but names."

"Don't worry about it Mitch, it's Joe. We met at the house where you installed new cabinets and I reclaimed the yard."

"Oh yeah, I remember. You were cursing at your hedge-trimmer because you couldn't get it started. And when you finally did, you ran out of gas fifteen minutes later. Then you were *really* pissed."

"You do have a good memory Mitch. I remember you had the key to the customer's storage shed and found some mixed-gas for me. It saved me time and money because that job was in the middle of no-where."

"It was about four years ago, in the spring, right?" Mitch said.

"Yeah, in April and I remember you were burnt out on the job. You had already been there a month and our customer kept piling on more work." It seemed Joe had a good memory as well. The reason his recollection was so vivid was something Mitch could not have prepared for. It was unimaginable.

"When you eventually started the hedge-trimmer you made short work of those shrubs. You have a real talent for pruning Joe, you should be proud of that."

"Thanks, Mitch, I take pride in my work because my old man taught me not to half-ass *anything*."

"So did mine," Mitch said. "He served in the infantry during the Korean War and was a real hard-ass when it came to work."

"I know what you mean Mitch. My dad served in Vietnam as a Green Beret. He did two tours from early 1966 through to the Tet offensive in '68."

"Jesus, I bet he saw hell over there," Mitch said.

"Yeah he did, but he never talked about it. I remember when he came back; I was just a little kid maybe four or five. He would wake up in the night, screaming. I'll never forget that awful scream. I hate what Vietnam did to my dad. I never got to know 'the real man' because of Vietnam."

Joe and Mitch looked out the window at the busy road. Cars sped by with the familiar sound of rubber tires swishing through wet pavement. A sound so common in the Northwest winters it often fell on apathetic ears. Rain caused droplets of water to find their intermittent path down the window. It resembled a transparent maze. Mitch wanted to lecture Joe on what he thought about Vietnam, but realized this was *not* the time. Joe needed someone to vent his frustration too now.

"If it means anything, I want you to know I appreciate your father's service to our country." Mitch said.

"It means *something* Mitch and the same goes for your dad."

"He didn't serve long in Korea, but was proud of his contribution. When he got back he didn't get the rousing reception other veterans did after World War II. Years later the conflict in Korea would be known as 'the forgotten war.' My dad hated that, he really did. That was nothing compared to what your dad must have gone through."

"Like I said, Mitch, he didn't say much except he hated war and people who would burn the flag or talk bad about him and his buddies, calling them baby killers. Can you believe how stupid some people are?"

"Yes I can, Joe. It reminds me of a bumper sticker I saw once."

"Oh yeah, what did it say?"

"*There's no cure for stupid.*"

Mitch and Joe enjoyed their first good laugh. Joe came in on Sundays and Mitch on Saturdays so they never ran into each other, until today. They had a lot in common: Both ran their own business and worked with their hands. Both fathers had served during wartime. And both men had suffered. What Mitch could not have known was the dark secret Joe carried around since they met.

"So, Mitch, I've never seen you here on a Sunday, is this a fluke?"

"Kind of, my mom is sick today and she didn't want me to get sick visiting her. So I came here. I was the first customer through the door and it has already been a strange day."

"Why?" Joe asked as he took off his coat and sat it beside him in the booth. "I saw a girl I had seen here before and we started talking. Before you knew it, we shared our innermost secrets. She gave me her phone number, but I don't think I can call."

"Why not, Mitch, it sounds like you like her."

"Maybe I'll call her someday, but I'm afraid she doesn't like *me*."

"*Someday* never comes, Mitch."

"I guess so. What brings you in here today, Joe, you look a little down."

"Yeah it's a dark anniversary for me today; I guess I can't hide it very well. It happened a while ago, not too long before we met out at that jobsite."

"You mean four years ago?"

"Yes, Mitch, four years ago *today*."

Mitch's mind raced, wondering what happened four years ago. Should he ask? He decided to wait until Joe was ready.

"I don't know if you noticed, Mitch, but the day I met you out at the jobsite I was coming out of a two-month shock. My mind was numb and my body on auto pilot. It was late-April with the cherry blossoms in full bloom. Our customer, the Nelsons, have at least a dozen cherry trees and that year, the blooms were late, but spectacular. I remember the sun shining through the trees onto bright pink petals on the lawn. You wanna know something funny, I didn't want to rake them up. They looked beautiful on the grass. From a distance it looked as though the petals resembled pink snowflakes melting on the grass. Pink was my sister's favorite color.

"Her casket was pink. I never cared for that color before she died but now, I need it. It soothes me. When I picked up the petals I could feel her with me. I could hear her voice: 'It's okay to let me go, Joe.' It's the hardest thing for me to do sometimes, *let things go*. She gave me permission and I started to let go. But I was still mad at her."

The two men looked at each other and then around the coffee shop. It wasn't as crowded, but many people were still engaged in conversation. To Mitch and Joe they were a silent movie, inaudible, moving their arms and hands like puppets. Joe had just described accurately what Mitch observed the day they met. But Joe was living it, the colors, the lighting and his sorrow. Both men agreed it was a beautiful day. Mitch was happy to be alive. Joe was struggling to go on.

"I want you to know Mitch; I really appreciate you helping me out. You had no idea how much I was suffering, yet you still went out of your way."

"It was the least I could do. I know how it is to run a business on your own. It's hard and lonely. I empathize with you Joe, as far as running a business goes. I respect any man who has the balls to go out there and make a living with his hands. I saw the work you did. It was immaculate. And the fact you did it while grieving for your sister is exceptional. Remember, Joe, no matter what *anyone* says, you have a purpose."

"Thanks Mitch, I'm glad I came here today."

Joe smiled and that made Mitch smile. He could tell Joe was struggling—struggling for the right words. Mitch was determined to stay. He could sense Joe needed him.

"Do you mind if I ask what happened to your sister Joe?"

"I don't mind, Mitch, but do you really want to know?"

Mitch contemplated that statement. He was prodding. He did not appreciate it when other people did this and now *he* was. By the nature of Joe's response Mitch realized something *horrible* must have happened. Joe looked out the window. The gray sky illuminated his blue cold eyes and sad face as he spoke.

"My wife and I were on our way back from Ocean Shores the day my sister died. You can get a room there real cheap in the wintertime. It was February 29th but still cold. We both love the ocean. It was a blustery, stormy morning like today and it looked like the ocean was angry. I knew something was wrong. Just one of those feelings you get, but don't why.

"When we arrived in Bellevue there was a message on my landline. My aunt called leaving a strange message. There's no cell phone coverage out near the ocean where we stayed, so she couldn't reach me. It wasn't until hours later when I retrieved the frantic cell phone messages that I really woke up. The message on my landline said, 'Joe, call home, call home, NOW!' I listened to the message another five times trying to understand what it meant. I picked up the phone to call my parents wondering who would answer. When my aunt answered I could hear my mom yelling at my father in the background. She kept yelling at my father telling him there was nothing he could have done for her! "*Nothing he could have done for her*," what did it mean? Who was my mom talking about? My aunt spoke in a loud, calm voice. She told me my sister and her baby were dead.

"It wasn't until after I retrieved the cell phone messages left right after my family had heard the news that I could hear the horror in my aunt and parents' voices. After they realized my sister killed herself and took the baby with her, I heard yelling, crying, grief, confusion and sorrow I cannot erase from my memory."

Mitch avoided eye contact. He kept looking down at the table as Joe looked out the window. Joe's sister and her baby kept going through his mind. It didn't matter to Mitch how they died. Who cares? They're dead and Joe and his family were left to suffer. This is what Mitch believed. Believed that is, until he heard *how* they died.

"Jesus, Joe, I'm so sorry, I never knew."

"It's okay, Mitch, I mean, how could you know? I don't talk about it much anymore. I learned the hard way, that is, trying to explain to people what happened, and why. When I met you I was still in shock.

Then I felt guilty. Maybe there was something I could have done. Then I was mad all the time. Not just at her, but everyone, especially God. When my anger started to fade I became depressed. I couldn't describe it as *normal* depression. This was different. I had no control over it. I've always tried to have a positive attitude. But after my sister *killed herself*, I didn't care. I didn't fucking care anymore."

Mitch still looked down at the table. He couldn't look Joe in the eyes. He felt like a coward. He didn't know what to say. Mitch always had an answer, like his father. He could analyze almost any situation and come up with a solution. If he could not resolve the problem based on personal experience he would at least try to make others feel better. For this reason, Mitch gravitated toward elders. Anyone who lived through the Great Depression could relate to almost *any* problem. Unfortunately, Mitch did not have an answer for suicide—the silent killer.

Mitch acquiesced to the tension and blurted out the first question that popped in his mind.

"Did you ever find out why Joe, *why* she did it?"

"I have been asked a thousand times and the answer is always the same. There's only one person who knows the real reason. She is dead. When I go to the cemetery, I ask her why: The answer, *silence.* I'm surprised you haven't asked me about the baby. *Everyone* wants to know about her baby."

"Joe, I do want to ask, but I'm afraid of your answer."

Mitch had blocked the baby out of his mind. He

could not comprehend the overwhelming loss. What about Joe's parents? They lost a child *and* grandchild in the same instant. Mitch began to wonder if coming into this coffee shop today was a mistake. He wanted to help Joe, but how? What words could soothe this humble man?

Mitch always questioned God's influence over men: But what about a baby? Why couldn't God save an unborn baby? Joe's horrific story left Mitch wondering if God *really* helps children or anyone. He understood why Joe was mad at God. He had a right, a god damn right!

"I haven't told the whole story to anyone Mitch. I didn't know how. It's been four years now and it's time I got it off my chest. Some things still bother me, or should I say haunt me."

"What things Joe? You can tell me if you feel up to it."

"I am, Mitch, but only if you are."

"I am and don't worry, I will keep what is said here today to myself, not that I would know how to describe it to anyone."

"Now you know how I feel, Mitch."

The two men shared a quick laugh: Quick, because there is *nothing* funny about suicide. Mitch was glad Joe was comfortable enough to share this tragedy with him. Joe trusted him. Mitch could not betray that trust.

The clouds broke apart just enough to reveal a glimpse of sun. This happened a lot more than anyone from Seattle remembered during the winter. It seemed everyone remembered the dark and rainy days in February, but forgot the brief aperture of sunlight between the melancholy gray. The pavement outside began to steam from the mild heat as Joe and Mitch looked out the window.

"It's so bright," Mitch said as the sun filled the coffee shop with golden light.

"The sun looks angry to me since my sister died. I know that sounds weird, but it looks different—*angry through the trees*. That's how I feel when I see the sun set through the trees, angry." Mitch now looked intently at Joe's face. The description of anger was mirrored on his face. So compelling was this story even Mitch felt an uncontrollable rage. He clenched his fist for about thirty seconds and then reached across the table as his hand opened slowly. Mitch put his right hand on Joe's left shoulder and for the first time that day he looked Joe square in the eyes: "You've got a *right* to be angry."

"Thanks, Mitch, I appreciate your honesty. That's the thing I noticed about you when we first met and it means a lot to me. It's still hard for me to talk about this. You would think after four years it would get easier. It doesn't. It just exposes more questions with no one to answer them. It's hard for me to talk about the baby. I don't know how to explain it to people."

The sun moved behind clouds again as Joe tried to summon the strength to finish. The earth seemed sad. Everyone in the coffee shop seemed happy, except these two men. One recalled a nightmare from which he could not wake up. The other listened—absorbed by the moment and wanting the moment to end.

"My sister had beautiful long-blond wavy hair. I have dreams about her boy and what he might have looked like. In my dream he is walking around the cemetery where they are buried. It's always the same dream, a bright sunny day and a cute little boy with wavy blond hair wandering around the graveyard aimlessly. In the dream he is smiling and looks happy.

"I wake up when he finds their gravestone and points at his name. It's strange waking up from a nightmare into another nightmare, except the waking nightmare is *real*. It seems inconceivable, something your mind wants to comprehend, but at the same time to forget, or worse, shut down altogether. I think that's what I've done, shut down. He would be almost four years old now and discovering his identity. But she took it all away; her identity, his identity, my family's identity and mine. Now there's just a hole, where there was once love. Suicide leaves an indelible brand on the survivors. It *cannot* be erased."

Mitch looked down at the table again. What could he say? Now was no time to panic. He was here for a reason and he had better figure that out, *now*. Joe needed him. Mitch asked Joe if he could share a story about a friend he knew in high school that died in a similar way.

"I cannot imagine the *horror* you and your family have had to endure. It must be hard on your parents. I've heard the worst thing any parent can go through is the loss of a son or daughter. But to lose a daughter and grandson in one day, Jesus, it's just not fair Joe. I'm so sorry."

"Thanks, Mitch, I can tell you've lost someone in the past."

"Really, how?"

"You said you were sorry when most people just ask why. I hate when people ask me that. I feel like telling them; I'll let you know when I can talk to the dead."

"I'm sorry I asked, Joe, I should've known better."

"Don't worry, Mitch, at least you showed some sincerity. Most people just ask why and then want some morbid *sick* answer. Fuck 'em all! Ask *their* God for answers because when it comes to suicide, I don't have any."

"I don't think they know *what* to say Joe. Instead of saying they're sorry they just ask questions."

"They do almost every time Mitch."

"I'm sure most of them mean well, but I've had enough people die on me to try not to ask. Isn't having someone you love *die*, hard enough?"

"It's enough," Joe said.

"I had some friends I knew in high school who drank and did drugs and some died. In fact, five died in one year, most of them from drugs or drinking and driving. I was seventeen and going to a funeral almost every other month. My mother warned me if I didn't straighten up, I would be next. That scared the shit out of me. I didn't even try to get my driver's license until I was nineteen. It was the late seventies and it seemed every dude had a muscle car but me.

"One of my friends and I were real close. His name was Raymond and my mom adored him. I was a senior and Raymond a junior, but I was only two months older. Anyway, Raymond had the most intense eyes and personality of anyone I've met. My mother told me he was a good dresser and better looking than me. I hated that. Raymond was a crazy driver; I mean this guy did the stupidest shit on the road. I told him, 'You're going to get killed one of these days.' He drove a tiny Toyota Corolla. This car had *no* protection.

"One day at school Raymond asked me if I would cut class so we could go cruise around with two other friends. I'd told him no because if I cut class the teacher would kick me out for good. I wouldn't have enough credits to graduate. I'm not kidding, Joe, I was a real fuck-up in high school. Raymond was pissed and called me a few choice names. I lost it and told him to get the hell away from me. It was the last time I saw him alive."

"Jesus Mitch, what happened to him?"

"Well, he picked up a couple other guys I knew, but not close friends, I mean not like Raymond. They drove away and about ten minutes later, Raymond pulled right out in front of a dump-truck loaded with gravel. The sun was in his eyes and he couldn't see. He asked the other guys in the car if he should go for it. They said yes and he pulled that tiny car right in front of 60,000 pounds of moving rock and metal. Raymond and one other guy died, not right away but ..."

"It's okay Mitch, you don't have to finish."

"No I want to; I have not talked about this. I want to now, if you don't mind."

"I don't mind, Mitch, but you can stop any time."

Mitch couldn't stop because he had waited to tell someone what happened when he was so young— something he could not talk about until now.

"One guy barely survived. His name was Andy and he was a real quiet nice guy. I ran into him at a party that summer about six months after the accident. He told me the whole story. Andy was one of most humble guys I knew in high school, and he was forced to watch his buddies die."

"What do you mean *forced* Mitch?"

"When Andy started to talk about the accident he couldn't stop until he finished. *I* could not stop him. He knew Raymond and I were tight. I think it was important for him to tell me. I don't think he shared this with anyone, but me. It's strange looking back now, but I think Andy said more to me that night at the party than he did the entire time we went to high school. Andy was always so quiet, until that night.

"He said he was trapped in the passenger side of the car with the steering wheel wrapped around his neck facing his friends while watching the last few minutes of their lives. He tried to keep his eyes shut, but could not. When the ambulance, police and fire-fighters arrived he heard them talking. One of them said there was no way anyone could still be alive in Raymond's car. It looked like a huge smashed beer can. Andy was in shock, but managed to yell, 'HEY, I'M STILL ALIVE!' That got everyone's attention and the fire-fighters slowly peeled the twisted metal back until they reached him. Meanwhile, Andy watched the last moments of Raymond and David."

"Oh God, that poor guy. What did you say Mitch?"

"I didn't know what to say. I was young and inex-perienced. I just listened as the party got louder. But even over loud music and talking I heard Andy's soft-spoken words. I was mesmerized by his recollection, methodically recalling every gruesome detail. I knew he would never forget. It was sad to hear how my best friend died. And believe me Joe; I can still hear Andy's voice. I kept repeating: 'I'm sorry Andy, I'm sorry.' Like some scratched record stuck on a song you hate and yet keeps repeating . . . .

"I never saw Andy again. I had graduated and Andy would be a senior that year, just like Raymond, had he lived. I don't even know if he's still alive. What I do know is, the pictures he put in my mind from his awful description of the accident are still there to-day—just as he described them nearly thirty years ago. It's as if I was there."

"You almost *were* there Mitch. Maybe that's why

you still think about it. Sounds like you've had a hard life, with so many friends dying."

"That's another thing I feel bad about."

"What's that, Mitch?"

"If I had cut the class and went with Raymond they could still be alive."

"How in the *hell* do you know that Mitch?"

"I know, believe me, I do. Raymond and I *were* tight. He was intense and could be a real asshole but so could I. The point is he *listened* to me. Whenever he drove like a madman I told him to slow down and mellow out. He bitched about it, but he *would* slow down. They were at a T-intersection and the sun was in his *eyes*. Andy and the other guy in the car David, were both passive. When Raymond asked: 'Should I go for it?' they just said '*Yeah*.' If I was there I would've rode shotgun and yelled: 'ARE YOU OUT OF YOUR FUCKING MIND?! YOU CAN'T SEE A GODDAMN THING! WAIT, UNTIL YOU'RE SURE IT'S SAFE!' And you know what Joe? Raymond would've listened to me. The other guys would've been in the back seat and said nothing. Besides, I was a senior and they were all still juniors. And I am anything but passive."

"I definitely agree Mitch. I think you've carried around this guilt for a long time. It's a hard thing to swallow when you're seventeen."

"Yeah, it's strange, It was like I was in a movie, playing a role that I played before by many people, yet they're all me. The ending is always the same. It feels preordained. I've always hated the saying 'everything happens for a reason.' After losing so many friends to drugs and drinking and stupid shit I thought it should be: 'A lot of things happen for *no reason.*'"

"I like that Mitch, can I use it?"

"Sure, Joe, you've earned it."

"Is this the guy you wanted to tell me about?" Mitch realized he had rambled again. He meant no harm. He wanted to take Joe's mind off his sister. That's not what Joe needed right now—Joe needed a friend—someone who would listen.

"I'm sorry I just got lost in the past and I couldn't stop. I'll just stop now and listen."

"No, no, it's okay Mitch, I understand. I think you needed to share it with someone."

"Yeah, I did. I suppose I never did let it go. I still think about Raymond and every time I do, I feel awful."

"That's understandable, Raymond died so young."

"No, it's not just that. I do feel bad he died young, but I yelled at him and told him to go away. That's what he did Joe, go away *forever.*"

"I know Mitch; it's a lot like my sister. I bet you wish you could have that moment back, but how could you know what would happen? Nobody can predict the future. Some people say they can, but I think that's bullshit. I don't believe *God* can tell the future. I mean, if he knows my next step then *why* take it? And if he does know, then how can anyone have a will of their own? Are we all just puppets? I can tell how much Raymond meant to you. I'm sure if the tables were turned and he was sitting here now he would say the same thing about you."

The coffee shop became quiet and almost empty. Joe and Mitch were so absorbed in each other's stories they hadn't noticed any change. It was 12:30 PM when Joe offered to buy Mitch lunch. "You've read my mind, Joe; I was just going to ask you the same thing."

OUTSIDE THE RAIN returned with the wind. Joe and Mitch's minds were numb from sharing so much pain and sorrow. At the same time they were glad, almost relieved they walked into the coffee shop this day. Was there a reason these men ran into each other? Was it fate? One thing was certain: After today Joe and Mitch would not be the same men as *before*.

"So, do they have anything good for lunch here, Mitch?"

"I gotta be honest with you Joe; I've never had lunch here before. I've never been in here on a Sunday. Saturdays yes, but *never Sunday*."

They made their way to the front counter where Kayla and Christy waited with smiles and questions. "You gonna have lunch, Mitch, you look hungry?" Kayla asked. Joe interrupted and informed the girls he was buying and if they had any good sandwiches. Mitch responded, "A sandwich sounds pretty damn good right about now, and maybe soup with crackers. You got any of that Kay?" Not wanting to be left out

Christy walked over to Joe and told him she would make them both sandwiches, *any* way they wanted.

"Now that's what I call service," Mitch said with a smile. "Sounds good, Christy, I'll have a roast beef on rye with Swiss cheese and tomatoes." Joe said looking *almost* cheerful. "Want any soup with that sir?"

"Sure I'll have whatever you've got." Joe wasn't a picky eater. That made *one* of them.

Mitch took his time to order. When he finally did; Joe and Christy thought they were in sandwich ordering hell. Lucky for Kay she was busy at the window serving customers because Mitch recited loudly how he wanted his sandwich and soup: "None of this, a little of that, and whatever you do, DO NOT put any tomatoes on it!"

"Okay, Mitch, settle down, no one here is going to sabotage your sandwich." Christy started to giggle and Mitch apologized. "I'm sorry; I got that from my dad. He used to be in the restaurant business for almost forty years, well let's just say, I am a lot easier customer than he was."

"You miss your dad, don't you Mitch?" Joe said with a somber look.

"Do you miss your sister, Joe?" Mitch said with a dead serious look.

"Okay Mitch, it was a stupid question. Anyone can tell how much you loved your father."

"And anyone can tell how much you loved your sister. But the *way* you lost her is indescribable. I can't imagine how your family must feel."

117

"Don't forget the baby, Mitch; I'm worried no one will remember the baby."

"Jesus, Joe, the baby. I'm so sorry." They quietly made their way back to the booth.

Christy arrived with the sandwiches and another smile. She sensed something was wrong.

"Are you two okay?"

"Yeah we're fine, just talking about friends and family members we've lost over the years," Mitch said.

"Oh, I've never known anyone who's died. I guess I'm just lucky." Joe stood up, grabbed the two plates loaded with sandwiches and soup and looked Christy in the eyes and said, "*Everyone* dies young lady." There was a quiet moment coinciding with a look of shock on Christie's face. She realized she'd made the wrong comment. To her, losing a family member was inconceivable. She was young and didn't want to think about death.

Joe and Mitch could remember a time in their lives when they were that way. When they were young and had all their friends and family around. Death seemed like a dream, and everybody wakes up from a dream. When a grandmother or grandfather dies, followed by an uncle and maybe some friends from school, death becomes real. Then the dream is over and it's time to wake up.

Christy struck a chord in Joe's mind. "She's never had anybody die. You hear that one Mitch?"

"Relax Joe, she's just a kid. She's being honest, probably doesn't know any better. I'm kind of jealous;

I mean she's so innocent. Nothing takes away innocence like death. Let her have it while it lasts."

"I suppose you're right Mitch. She probably thinks I'm weird for making that comment. When it does happen to her, I'll bet you a nickel she remembers what I said."

"I do too, especially the *way* you expressed yourself. It was intense."

"Okay, Mitch, maybe I went over the top. I'll apologize later. Like you said, she's just a kid. Say, you didn't tell me about your friend in high school, I mean the one that died like my sister."

"Okay I'll tell you but can we eat first, I'm starving."

As Joe and Mitch sat back down at the table to eat their lunch, Mitch noticed an elderly well-dressed English gentleman sitting across the room and staring at them. Mitch assumed he was English by the tea-bag clasp extending from the lid of his coffee cup. He *looked* English. Of course, the old English style hat hanging on the rack alongside the impressive bright-red scarf, suggested British attire.

There was something strange about this man. Mitch tried to ignore *the English gentleman* while he and Joe ate their lunch. When they finished, Christy, still baffled by Joe's harsh remark, carefully removed their plates with no expression.

"Look, Christy, I didn't mean to lay into you. You didn't deserve it, I apologize."

Christie's expressionless face lit back up.

"Thanks Joe, I'm sorry too, I mean for being so

insensitive."

"Glad to see you kids kiss and make-up," Mitch said with a grin. An almost simultaneous 'SHUT-UP MITCH!' came from Joe and Christy, but *all* were smiling. Christy took the dishes back to the kitchen as Mitch looked over at the old man sipping tea.

"Hey Joe, do you see the old guy over there? He's looking right at us. He's making me nervous."

"I think you were born nervous Mitch. Has anyone ever told you you're paranoid?"

"Yes to the first comment and almost everyone to the second. My paranoia has paid off."

"How's that Mitch?"

"I see things others don't. Therefore, I'm able to adjust and avoid mistakes."

"I believe that. A little paranoia is a good thing, but too much is a burden."

"Then I was born with a cumbersome burden."

"Aren't we all Mitch?"

Joe turned his head and waved to the old man. He raised his cup and nodded in reply. It was a gesture of respect from an old man to a young man.

"See, he nodded, looks like a nice old man to me Mitch. I think you're just making excuses not to tell your story. Forget the old guy and get on with it, I'm getting impatient Mitch."

"Are you sure you wanna hear this? I was hoping you'd forget it."

"No, I didn't forget. How could I? Anyway, *you* brought it up."

"Okay, okay, I'll tell you. This happened the year before all those guys I told you about died—when I was a junior in high school—when I was sixteen."

"I USED TO live about two miles from my high school. No buses stopped anywhere near my house, so every morning I hitchhiked to school. I hitchhiked a lot back then. I met a lot of interesting people and felt safe most of the time. I couldn't imagine hitchhiking these days.

"Back then I'd stick my thumb out on the way to school and watch the same people pass me by every day. This was the most difficult time of my life. No girlfriend, very few friends and practically no social life. I had bad acne that my mother gave me a hard time about. They say sixteen is the worst age for a boy. I don't know if that's true for every boy, but it certainly was for me.

"Anyway, almost every morning at the same time and spot I'd get picked up from a high school guy and his mother. It was weird. I don't even know why I bothered to hitchhike before they picked me up. I never got a ride until they came along anyway. I would have been better off to take a shortcut I knew and then wait, rather than waste all that time trying to get a ride. This guy's name was Russ and it was his mother's car. Russ sat in the passenger seat and always smiled and told me, 'Hop in the back, Mitch.' His mom was a nice, quiet woman and didn't persecute me for hitchhiking. I always thanked her for giving me a ride. That made Russ and his mom smile.

"Russ was a senior on the wrestling team. He *looked* like a wrestler, short, stocky and tough. It was strange that he was so quiet and soft-spoken. A lot like Andy, but super-strong. The kind of guy you never wanted to piss-off. Whenever I saw him in the hallway he'd smile and say: 'Hey Mitch, how ya doing?' Russ was a prince and everyone I knew at school liked him—even the stoners because sometimes he would come out to the parking lot and have a smoke with us. He didn't do that often because he wanted to maintain his *jock* status. Every time I saw him he looked happy.

"One day at my locker picking up books, a friend of mine says, 'Did you hear about Russ?' It's never good to hear that Joe, *never*. The news: Russ killed himself. Apparently, he took some bad acid and freaked out. Russ stabbed himself over and over. I don't think he ever took acid before. Maybe a friend talked him into it. He freaked-out and stabbed himself to death. This was another time I wished I could've been there to tell Russ it's okay to say no. When you take acid, you are gambling with your mind."

"I see why you didn't want to tell me this story. Mitch, it's awful."

"Yeah I know, but that's not the worst part Joe."

"I'm afraid to ask, but please finish."

"About a month went by and winter became

spring. I still hitchhiked every day, but did not get a ride. I hadn't seen Russ's mother drive by. In some ways this was a good thing. After all, what could I say to her?

"Then one day in the same spot where she and Russ used to pick me up, I saw her. She drove an old four-door, lime-green Dodge Dart, impossible to miss. I turned around, stuck out my thumb and there she was. This time she did not stop. She drove right by me; her lifeless eyes looked straight ahead with no expression on her face. It seemed as though all happiness had been sucked out of her. The passenger side that used to feature Russ's smiling face was empty. Now, I'm convinced she didn't even see me. I finally stopped hitchhiking to school; I mean what's the point? Russ and his mom were the only ones who ever picked me up anyway. Eventually, I avoided that area; I just couldn't take it anymore. Can I tell you something Joe?"

"What's that, Mitch?"

"Part of me hoped she would stop and pick me up. Then I could tell her how sorry I was and that Russ was a special person and how I missed him. Another part of me was *glad* she didn't pick me up because I would have to face her and witness her grief and sorrow. If she did pick me up I would be sitting in Russ's seat wondering if she would think of him. As soon as you told me about your sister I thought about Russ and his mother. Sometimes I wish I could go back to the time when Russ and his mom were smiling just as they pulled over to pick me up. Sure, I would be stuck back in the worst time of my life—but Russ would be *alive* and his mom would be happy."

Mitch turned around and saw the red LCD clock switch from 1:12 to 1:13 PM. This had already been an unforgettable day. He was relieved finally telling this story. It was something he had wanted to do for nearly thirty years. Mitch had some bad things happen when he was in high school, but foremost in his mind was Russ and Raymond: Two extraordinary boys who died too young. Joe now looked down and avoided eye contact. He couldn't believe what he was hearing. Here was someone who understood what he was going through. For the first time in a *long time,* Joe did not feel alone. The two men took a few deep breaths followed by a moment of silence.

"We have a lot in common, Mitch. I came in here today feeling sorry for myself. It hadn't occurred to me someone else was going through the same thing."

"That was a long time ago Joe, and I don't think my experience is anything like what you had to go through. Don't get me wrong, Russ was a prince and his mom, well she was *his* mom. It's not like she was my mom or he was my brother."

"But you remembered every detail, like it was yesterday. You even remembered the car they drove—the make—the model—everything. You remembered the look on her face after *thirty* years. I think Russ's suicide had a profound effect on you Mitch."

"How could it not? I was a sixteen-year-old kid trying to figure out who the hell I was. Then one day I find out the guy I've been hitching a ride with almost every morning stabs himself in the chest a dozen times. One day he's walking down the hallway asking me how I'm doing. The next he's gone. I believe I lost my innocence when I found out about Russ. So, you see Joe, it's not just as though I remember; it's more like, how could I forget?"

"I understand Mitch, believe me I do."

"I know Joe."

The two men shared another moment of somber silence. The coffee shop was now almost empty except for the old British man who Mitch was convinced was listening to every word. It didn't matter anymore. Maybe the old man could make some sense of it because to Mitch *nothing* made sense. It seemed like a lot of people he knew thrown into this world, suffered and died young. He was mad. Mad at what happened to him and Joe. Mad because they had *no* say in the matter.

Unfortunately, in their own selfish moment, those who complete suicide leave a mess for those they loved, to clean up. Mitch thought he let Joe down because he didn't have answers, only questions. Joe took a sip of water and extended both hands in the air and behind his neck for an extended stretch. He took another sip of water and looked straight into Mitch's eyes and started to speak.

"You made me realize something today. Four years ago today, my sister killed herself and her baby. Now, after hearing and seeing the look on your face as you described what happened to Russ and Raymond, I realize I will live with this the rest of my life. I know my family must feel the same way. The stigma of suicide leaves indelible scars. People tell me things will get better with time. I want to slap the shit out of everyone who says that to me.

"We used to have our Christmas party at my sister's house. She and her husband decorated everything—inside and out. They always had a huge Nobel-Fir tree donned with colorful lights and rare ornaments my sister had collected over the years. She loved Christmas and made everyone feel welcome. After she died the parties ended. It wasn't the only thing that ended—we all drifted apart. Christmas didn't have the same meaning anymore.

"Everyone looked at me differently after my sister died. Some of my customers and friends looked at me as though suicide was a contagious disease. Maybe they thought I had it and *they* could catch it. I lost business and friends. Even my wife looks at me like she's afraid. I believe we are drifting apart and there's nothing I can do. If my sister could see how much she took away from everyone *before* she killed herself, she would have decided to live. Unfortunately, her decision was final. She can't come back. No one can come back.

"I remember the first Christmas after she died. It was about a week before Christmas Day and I was at home alone, listening to Christmas music and singing along with the classics I grew up with. An instrumental version of 'What Child Is This?' started playing—a slow haunting rendition featuring violins and cellos that normally would lift my spirits. Then, it hit me. The child I was thinking about was my sister's unborn baby, just three weeks from coming into this world before my sister killed herself. I listened and wondered why this happened. I realized I would never know. I cried. It was the saddest moment of my life Mitch."

Mitch avoided eye contact. This time it was for different reasons. His eyes were welling up with tears. Joe was oblivious and couldn't stop talking until he released his pent up emotions.

"You know Mitch, all my life I've wondered what it would be like to have never been born. I know it sounds crazy, but it's how I feel. When I was a kid I wanted to make my mark on this earth. To be remembered for something. At the end of my life I could tell my grandchildren, 'Look, I made a difference, now it's your turn.' Sure, I've had my share of heartache and disappointment. I've made mistakes. Sometimes I complain and blame others for my problems. I've done some pretty shitty things in my life along with some good things. But at *least* I had my chance goddamn it!

"Every time I catch myself bitching about some-thing stupid I think of my unborn nephew. He never got the chance—to be born, to grow up, play baseball, fall in love, throw eggs at a car on Halloween. He never got the chance to hike up a mountain early one Sunday morning and yell at the universe: 'I MADE IT; I MADE IT TO THE TOP!' No matter how bad my life gets, at the end of the day at least I could say—I had a life. It's just so fucking unfair. I miss him—he was never born, but I still miss him, Mitch."

Mitch turned around and saw the red LCD clock showed 1:30 PM. The coffee shop started to get crowded again. Mitch wondered if the people coming in could ever comprehend or imagine what Joe was going through. After all, *how much is enough?* How much can a person take before going crazy? Isn't this life crazy enough? Add suicide into the mix and it's just too much. Mitch was amazed Joe seemed to be able to cope with all this.

Or *maybe* he wasn't coping. Mitch was afraid he would say something wrong and add to Joe's misery. Joe saw something in Mitch that made him feel it would be okay to share his story. It was a bridge of trust. Now, the bridge was overloaded and Mitch was worried it would crumble under the weight of grief. Mitch had to tread lightly.

"The way you describe your nephew it's no won-der you miss him." Mitch said with a trembling voice trying to hold back tears. "I mean, it's almost as if he were here with us. I feel I know him and at the same time, never being able to ever know him is sad. It kinda reminds me of the guys I knew in high school who died. But I at least had the chance to know them. I wonder who speaks for your nephew."

"No one speaks for him Mitch, my sister made damn sure of that and that's the reason why I'm still so fucking mad at her. For a while I thought I was okay with what happened. Since I started having those dreams about my nephew walking around the cemetery, my anger is almost uncontrollable. But I would rather be mad all the time than feel nothing at all."

The sadness on Joe's face now turned into rage. Was Mitch responsible for this? Every time he calmed Joe he would say something and start the cycle of sorrow and anger again. Mitch noticed a pattern developing. He could see it now. It was right there the whole time, but it wasn't until now that he understood what was happening. Mitch realized that he would either lift the weight of anger on Joe's back, or make a wrong step and cause the bridge to tumble down, burying Joe in despair. Mitch was tiptoeing across. But he just couldn't sit there and say *nothing*. He took a risk.

"I understand your anger Joe. What I'm about to say might make it worse, but I have to say it."

"Don't worry Mitch, I won't take a swing at you." The two men shared another laugh. However, Mitch was worried this new friendship would end before it ever got started.

But as a friend he needed to say it . . . .

"Have you ever considered forgiving your sister? No conditions, no expectations—just forgive. I know it sounds hard because you're still mad. Maybe that's what she needs now—everyone to forgive her. I might have no right to say it because I didn't know your sister, but I can tell how much you loved her. And if she loved you then 'forgiving her' is the one thing you *can* do. Sarah, the girl I met here earlier today told me the same thing about an ex-girlfriend I had. She noticed I was still mad. I think it's good advice. It's almost as if I *need* my anger. Sometimes I do need it, but should I be angry at someone who might be dead. How ridiculous is that?"

Mitch wanted to say more, but realized this was not the time. Joe took a long look out the window at the dark-gray skies and pondered what Mitch was saying. Mitch was worried the bridge of trust was crumbling.

"I've thought about it a lot Mitch. Maybe not in the way you described it, but I *have* thought about it. It bothers me, or should I say haunts me that I haven't forgiven her. I'm not ready. I know it doesn't make sense, but since she killed herself, not much does. How did you learn how to forgive?"

"I'm still learning how, but I remember when a friend of mine died after a long battle with cancer. His name was Gordon and we were close—closer than I was to my own dad at the time. When he found out he had cancer, it was already in the late stages. He did two tours in Vietnam. He was there during the Tet offensive, same as your dad.

"I met him at church about two years after I graduated from high school. It was near the end of my church-going and right before my dad kicked me out of the house. Looking back now I understand why he did it. We fought constantly and my mother wanted me out. I was just another smart-ass nineteen-year-old who thought I knew everything but didn't know shit. Gordon was in his early forties then and born the same day and *year* as John Lennon. The funny thing is he didn't care for The Beatles. He had no idea he was the same age as John until I told him.

"This was about a year and a half after John's tragic death and even though Gordon did not care for The Beatles he said: 'I can't believe anyone would shoot him. I didn't care much for his music, but at least he tried to promote peace. I respected that. At the time he was protesting the war lots of my buddies were still over there and didn't care for that. Now, I understand what he was trying to say. *Give Peace a Chance*, I like that.'

"I didn't point out he quoted a John Lennon song because I realized it wasn't the music he identified with. It was what the music was saying. I suppose that's why John Lennon was probably the most popular, yet misunderstood musical artist."

"I agree, Mitch. Just listen to *Imagine*, only a fool or an idiot would try to remake that song."

"He would have to be a fool *and* an idiot," Mitch said thinking how John died.

"I remember when he died," Joe interjected. "I was just fifteen, but I could tell from the look on my dad's face after he heard the news that someone special had died. It was almost as if a family member had died. Anyway Mitch, get back to this Gordon guy."

"Well, one of Gordon's duties was to spray Agent Orange to kill the foliage. Can you believe it? The assholes running that war had no idea what they were doing. I don't think they even cared about exposing the men fighting to toxic chemicals. Anyway, he fought the cancer for almost four years. He went through everything: chemotherapy, radiation treatment and even the so called magic-bullet treatment toward the end.

"They even tried a bone-marrow transplant that was eventually matched up to a brother he hadn't seen in eight years. Back then you had to have an exact genetic match. It was bizarre, nobody could find this guy. Then, out of the blue he comes forward and gives Gordon another chance. The operation worked and gave Gordon another two years. The cancer came back. He became another casualty in the aftermath of that pointless war.

"His funeral was very emotional for me. He died just before Christmas when a thick fog seemed to linger and absorb everyone's sorrow. Even the pastor mentioned how the fog had come and took Gordon to heaven. This old pastor's words hit me the hardest."

"What did he say Mitch?"

"Well, let me describe this man. He was a short, older, balding man who wore dark-framed glasses. I think he was Irish. That's the funny part about it. Gordon was Lutheran and we were at a Lutheran church and here was this guy with an Irish accent. It was weird. I grew up Catholic and this guy looked Catholic. Anyway, I met this pastor before a few times. He always gave me a funny look—like he knew something no one else did. It was strange; he made me nervous and knew it."

"Wait a minute; I thought you said you were Catholic? What were you doing at a Lutheran church?"

"Oh yeah, I got tired of all the praying penance to Mary, not being able to eat meat on a Friday, sacrificing your firstborn Catholic bullshit. Don't get me going on this subject ..."

"Okay Mitch, I was just wondering."

"Sorry about that, Joe. I didn't mean to take it out on you, but you can see I have some *issues* with the Catholic Church. Although, I should admit there was a young priest who helped me through a difficult time going through high school. And, I never had problems with priests touching me where they shouldn't. But I wasn't an altar boy like my brothers so I can't speak for *all* boys. My brothers never told me anything ever happened to them, but if it did, I don't think anyone would believe them. Back then the priests and nuns had *absolute* authority over us kids. So, when I hear all the shit coming out now about molestation, it doesn't surprise me. If you were a kid at my school and you came home saying *anything* derogatory about any priest or a nun—you were dead meat."

"So I take it you tried a Lutheran church for a while," Joe said hoping Mitch would settle down. "Yeah, just want to see if I was missing something."

"So what did the older pastor say?" Joe asked to get Mitch back on track.

"Everyone had the opportunity to say some final words, then goodbye. I didn't say anything. I wanted to—I really *wanted* to say something, *anything* but I couldn't find the words. The old pastor spoke last. 'I know many here today feel sad. Some of you may feel angry. It's okay to be mad—it's even okay to be mad at God. Gordon battled cancer with dignity and pride. Unfortunately, at times he must've been difficult to be around. Some people here who were very close to him may have exchanged harsh words and now have feelings of regret or guilt. I would like to say to all those here today that feel that way: Forgive Gordon and then yourself.'

"I must tell you, Joe, every time I looked up that old priest was staring right at *me*."

"God, that's weird," Joe said.

"He knew something, I don't know *how* he knew but he did. About two months before Gordon died we had a fight and exchanged harsh words. I don't know why I couldn't let it go. I said some pretty shitty things I still feel bad about. We didn't talk for about a month and then he invited me to dinner. After dinner, he took me into his garage and told me I could have anything I wanted after he was gone. There was a moment of somber silence. He looked so weak and skinny. His face was thin and his eyes were tired. He knew he would die soon and here he was, offering me his stuff. Somehow I managed to hold back the tears, but it was hard. I didn't want to cry in front of him. Gordon had accepted his fate. He took me into his garage to say goodbye."

"Jesus, Mitch, what did you say?"

"I told him not to give up hope. I was only twenty-three and still thought anything was possible. Even though I could see it in his eyes, I hoped and prayed for a miracle. We didn't talk about the fight we had. Instead, I said I loved him and he was like a second father. I was scared. Then he shook my hand the *same* way he shook my hand the first time I met him and said, 'Don't worry about me Mitch, I'll be okay, in this life and the next. I'm proud of you Mitch, proud to call you my friend.' I reached my limit. I cried right there in his garage until he grabbed me and told me we should eat dinner. It was the last meal we had together. Gordon died a month later."

It was Joe's turn to observe the heartache he thought until now, was reserved for him. But he was wrong. This time the expression on Mitch's face spoke to him. It wasn't until this moment Joe realized how much pain Mitch had in his heart—how much pain someone else carried around each day. It didn't make him feel better about his sister's death and the nightmare of her baby, but it did make him pause and understand he wasn't the *only* one suffering.

Joe thought about all the people he had met since his sister died. How many of *them* were going through the death of a brother, sister, mother or father? He felt guilty knowing the pain in the faces of the nameless strangers he'd met on the train, in the grocery store or just walking down the street and not acknowledging it. He was too busy confirming his own pain; he didn't want or even care to accept pain in others. Mitch helped Joe to accept what happened to his sister. He would *never* agree with it, but he could accept it. With that acceptance, maybe he could forgive her.

The wind outside began to pick up again. Joe and Mitch watched as a nearby traffic light did its dance to the wind. They both felt like that traffic light— getting knocked around in this life, yet yielding to its constant changes. As they watched the light turn from green to yellow and finally red, they were reminded of the friends and family they had lost. The traffic light colors highlighted the ups and downs and pauses in this journey we call life. For both men, this was indeed a day for pause and understanding.

"Maybe you're right Mitch. I've thought about it many times, but I just can't seem to let it go."

"Let what go, Joe?"

"My anger, my bitterness, I can't let them go. But I must. After today I know I *have* to let go. If I don't my sister's memory will always haunt me in a negative way. Now, *maybe* I can turn that negative energy into something positive. I have to do something different because being mad all the time is not working. You've made me realize something my father has tried to tell me since she died."

"What's that Joe?"

"After my sister's suicide, we all went to my parents' house. All my siblings and some of my aunts and uncles were there. Everyone was in shock, crying and asking: why did she do this—how could she do this? My mother kept saying, 'This is the worst thing that could ever happen to a family.' I asked my father what he thought happened to her. I will not forget his response. 'She just got sick and died son.' He told me that four years ago today, but I don't believe I fully understood what he meant until now."

"What do you think he meant Joe?"

"Eventually, he explained it to me in a more practical way. About three months after she died my parents asked me if I wanted to go to a peer-led grief group called: Survivors of Suicide or SOS for short. Each meeting was emotional turmoil. We would all sit around a big table; state our names and the loved ones we had lost to suicide.

"The leader of the group, Brian, had a son who attempted suicide *the first time* and was unsuccessful. He took some pills and ended up in a wheelchair. Brian and his wife had to keep him under constant surveillance. Anyway, about a year after his first attempt, he tried it again. This time he died. He used a gun, like my sister did. When someone wants to end their life you know they're serious if they use a gun. Never mind messing around with pills or jumping off a bridge or slitting your wrist—those methods are unreliable. If you use a gun, it means you're goddamn serious about dying."

"These meetings sound intense, Joe."

"Yes they were, but the hardest part was watching new people come in after I had been there a while. I mean to see the look of shock and disbelief on their faces was devastating. I went to these meetings for about three years and they really helped me. But I never got used to seeing the looks on the mothers' and fathers' faces explaining what happened to their sons or daughters. That was tough. And they all would say the same things: 'If I just could have been there for him' or 'I should've seen it coming.' That's how I felt the first few months after my sister died.

"We all felt that way, but the reality is, once someone gets in that dark space and makes up their mind, *nothing* or no one can stop them. They're in a *black hole* of despair where gravity has taken hold of their pain and won't let go. They want to feel better, but don't know how. Finally, when they make the decision to erase their presence from this earth, they feel an overwhelming sense of joy knowing their suffering will end. Suicide is a permanent answer to a temporary problem."

"Is that what your dad said about your sister?"

"He put it a different way, Dad said ..."

"Suicide will kill you the same way as heart disease or cancer. There's no difference. If somebody dies from a heart attack there's no question *how* they died. With suicide everyone wants to know what happened—why did they do this—how could they do this? It doesn't matter how or why. All that matters is they were sick. So sick they died."

"I still try to explain it in some profound way. Nothing I come up with compares with the simple answer my father gave the day she died. My dad has a gift with words no one else I know has."

"It sounds like it Joe, I think you're lucky to call him Dad."

"I love him Mitch and I do feel fortunate."

Mitch turned around and saw 2:15 PM on the red clock. Both men did their best to hold back tears. They crossed the bridge together and made it to the other side. Behind them was a legacy of *life* and *death*. There was no going back—no need to go back. Mitch helped Joe to forgive someone that just one day ago seemed improbable. Joe helped Mitch understand the importance of family and how fast things can be taken away. Both men looked out the window as the cars went by and wondered where life would take them after today . . . .

The coffee shop had a few new people who looked into the void of their laptop screens. Christy finished her shift and waved goodbye to Mitch and Joe. It was 2:30 PM now and the noon rush was over. Kay would be fine on her own. Mitch yelled, "THAT WAS SOME

AWESOME COFFEE BABY!" Christy yielded one more self-conscious smile and opened the door to the sound of that familiar dull ring. Mitch hadn't heard the bell ring the entire time he talked with Joe. Just as with Sarah, he had been taken out of the present and put in a different place. This was unusual for Mitch because he was normally aware of everything going on around him. Today was different.

"Well Mitch, it has certainly been real."

"Yes it has, Joe. Do you have to go now?"

"Yeah, I gotta head over to Bellevue and do a bid on a job before dark. Some lady wants me to rip up everything in the backyard and start from scratch."

"That's good, sounds like a lot of work."

"It's all good, until I give her the price, then it's: 'Let me talk to my husband,' or 'I'll get back to you.' The *polite* way for a woman to say no."

"I know what you mean, Joe, I've heard some pretty strange things too. At least with a man you can negotiate if the price is too high. With a woman, if the price too high it's almost always, 'Thanks for coming out,' or as you said, 'I'll get back to you.'"

Another laugh, let out by two men that would be linked together in a way no one but themselves would understand. They exchanged business cards in hopes of staying in touch. Like so many other things in life, it didn't work out. Joe moved to California where he could work year round. Mitch tried to get a hold of him a few times, but was unsuccessful. They would not see or talk to each other again after today—the last day of February in a leap year.

"Well Joe, it was nice talking with you. I don't know what your plans are for the rest of your life, but I do want you to know I will always remember you. I will mention you in my prayers."

"Thanks, Mitch, I appreciate it. Do you remember when I told you about my father and how I said there was no one else like him?"

"Of course I remember Joe, why?"

"Well as it turns out I was wrong, you're a lot like him Mitch. I think that's the reason I was able to trust you and tell you so much. You have a gift Mitch. Don't ever forget it."

"I don't know how to respond to that, except to say thank you and goodbye."

"Goodbye, Mitch."

The two men stood up and Joe put on his coat. They give each other a firm handshake and Joe went over to retrieve his hat from the coat rack. As he put on his hat, the old English gentleman walked over said a few words to him. They were just out of earshot so Mitch could not hear what they said. The old man pointed over at Mitch and said something to Joe. Mitch was very self-conscious because that old guy made him nervous. Joe headed toward the door, looked over at Mitch one more time and waved goodbye. A young couple rushed in from outside dinging the bell loudly. Just before the door closed, Joe turned his body, and quickly slid through before it closed. Mitch turned back around just in time to see the old fellow tip the cup to his mouth.

FOUR

I USED TO BE A SOLDIER

ITCH RUSHED INTO THE BATHROOM FOR A much-needed pee. While relieving himself he couldn't help think how *fragile* this life is. Joe forced him to confront his own mortality and confirmed how much he needed to be there for his mother. Every time Joe brought up *his* dad Mitch thought of his own father and how much he missed him. Mitch was also reminded of his family and how he had lost contact with so many aunts and uncles and even siblings.

Mitch's isolated sorrow sometimes exposed a cold, remorseless man, uncomfortable in his own skin— stuck with no way out. Fortunately, he did not feel that way often. When he did, he was helpless, like a crying baby with no mother to nurture it. Joe's story, as sad as it was, gave him encouragement. He had helped Joe to forgive. That helped Mitch to forgive.

Mitch washed his hands with soap and hot water and then frantically pushed down the paper towel dispenser until he had at least two feet of paper towel. He dried his hands methodically and flicked the wadded paper towel into the open garbage can, raised his hands and clenched both fists. The shot was good. He lightly tapped down on the handle that automatically unlocked the door and walked out. To the left, Kay sat at the counter lost in her magazine enjoying a break from her busy day. With the rush over, she would only serve a few more customers before the coffee shop closed at 6:00 PM.

To Mitch's right he could see the bottom of the spiral staircase. After he and Sarah exited the room upstairs where young lovers congregate, it became more inviting. Mitch turned left to take another look at Kay and then to the right at the base of the spiral staircase and decided to walk straight ahead back to his booth. He took a few steps and looked up. The old English gentleman looked straight at him with his mouth open and squinty eyes, peering into Mitch's psyche. Mitch looked at the old man then headed right for the stairs. "I can't take him staring at me anymore," he said to himself. He ascended the spiral staircase for the second time that day.

He was almost to the top when he saw the sun stream through the bottom of the door. This was strange because the room just had *one* tiny rectangular window. Mitch realized not only had the sun found its way out of the clouds again, the earth's near-spring tilt on its axis had positioned the sun in the exact trajectory of that tiny window. Mitch stood there for a minute as the sun gleamed off the shiny hardwood floor.

He heard some giggling and noticed two small feet on the left side from under the door silhouetted by the bright sun moving toward two larger feet from the right side. The smaller feet from the left met the larger feet from the right almost in the middle of a one inch brightly lit gap at the door bottom. Mitch saw the smaller set of feet (presumably the girl's) stand up on her tiptoes followed by more giggling. Through a *one-inch* gap at the door bottom, Mitch witnessed the perpetual romantic game young lover's play. Instead of feeling alone or even a little jealous he just turned around, smiled and walked back down the stairs, leaving the young couple undisturbed.

When he reached the bottom of the stairs Mitch decided it might be time to leave. After all, he had already stayed longer at the coffee shop today than ever before. After the experience with Joe his mind needed rest. He made a beeline to his booth to grab his worn coat and hat. The old man got up from his table and walked over.

"Do you mind if I have a word with you young man?" the old fellow said with a distinct gravelly British accent. Mitch's assumption was correct. He was indeed British and Mitch was compelled to accept this request.

"I don't mind," Mitch said wondering what this

was about. "I overheard some of your conversation with that other young man and wanted to tell you something." Then Mitch remembered the old guy mumbled something to Joe. "I just wanted to say I think you both are remarkable young men. I told your friend the same thing just before he left in case you're wondering." With this secret revealed Mitch's full attention was now on this peculiar man.

"My name is Leo Wolf," he said and extended his right hand out from under an overcoat hanging on the same arm. Mitch hadn't noticed he had picked up his things from the coat rack. "Do you mind if I sit down?"

"Not at all," said Mitch realizing his plans to leave had been foiled. The old fellow proceeded to carefully lay out his coat and hat followed by a red scarf over the empty bench in a methodical, organized manner. Mitch wondered why he went through all the trouble to remove his stuff from the coat rack—only to move it over to Mitch's booth and decorate the bench chair. Mitch was fascinated by his slow movements—each move had purpose. He made himself as comfortable as possible in the worn, semi-cushioned bench seat.

He was dressed in a neat, thick, light-gray tweed suit, yellow shirt, with a dark blue tie. A rather large nose protruded from his wrinkled distinguished face. A dark purple birthmark about the size and shape of an egg indelibly marked the left side of his lower neck. His forehead was large and angled sharply back to reseeding thin white hair on the top, but was still thick on the sides. A dull gold wedding ring on his left hand finger was so tight it seemed to cut off the circulation. He reached into an inner vest pocket and pulled out glasses, opening the wire frame, first the left then right and pulled them slowly to his face. He slid them back until they locked over large thick protruding ears.

"I hope you don't mind me eavesdropping in on the conversation with your friend. I'd tried not to listen, but couldn't help myself."

"How long were you listening Mr. Wolf?"

Mitch's father taught him from a young age to address older adult men and women as Mr. or Mrs. Attending Catholic school merely enforced Dad's rule. Mitch even addressed his customers with a "yes Ma'am" or "yes Sir" until he was comfortable enough, (or at their request) call them by their first name. When it came to the elderly there were *no* excuses— they were to be treated with respect.

"I appreciate your manners young man, but I would prefer if you called me by my first name, Leo. I know your name is Mitch because I heard your friend Joseph say it many times. I hope you don't mind if I just call you Mitch."

"Of course I don't mind, as long as you don't mind me calling you Sir or Mr. Wolf. You see, I was taught at a young age to respect elders."

"Fair enough young man or should I say, Mitch."

Mitch was impressed with this gentleman's elegant demeanor. Here he was asking Mitch if he could call him by his first name. Mitch was not used to this type of polite behavior.

"So *how long* were you listening?"

"Let's just say long enough to understand both of you have been through a great deal; especially at such a young age; a good deal more than most—at any age." The old man pulled out a vanilla colored handkerchief and blew his nose with a loud trumpet sound.

"Did you hear what happened to his sister?" Mitch said wondering how much the old man knew, but more importantly, understood what he was *really* getting into.

"I heard Joseph mention she died, but I did not hear how."

Just to see if the old man was certain he wanted to talk, Mitch decided to let him have it. Give him the truth and see how he reacts.

"She killed herself, took a gun and shot herself. And you wanna know the real kicker old man, she was just three weeks shy of giving birth to a baby boy."

"Dear God ... oh ... my dear God."

Mitch's blunt description of Joe's tragedy surprised even him. Here he was talking to a stranger about someone else's atrocious story. Mitch understood what was happening. He too was furious about what happened to Joe. Mad at what Joe's sister did and how she took so much with her when she died. Just took everything away. Mitch did not want to talk anymore. The old man deserved better.

"You look rather upset young man, perhaps this

was a mistake. It's my fault; I shouldn't have listened in on other people's private conversation," Mr. Wolf said as he started to rise up from the booth as though he were ready to leave.

"I'm sorry Sir; I didn't mean to come off like that. After listening to Joe's story I feel I've changed," Mitch said nervously tapping the table. This got the old man's attention so he sat back down and decided to stay.

"You have changed because you're growing. You will continue to grow until the day you die. You're lucky because some people *never* change or grow up. They wander through their lives thinking the world owes them something. Some of them die bitter and alone while others just go through the motions hoping things will change. Things *do* change, but sometimes the best things in life get swept away, while the *worst* remain."

The old man had Mitch's interest. Somehow, today, Mitch had lost some awareness of what went on around him. He could not believe what he heard today, and here, sitting in front of him was not only a man with deep convictions, but a man *with a story*. Mitch and Mr. Wolf decided to stay.

The old man and Mitch sat at the booth where Mitch and Joe sat. Mitch turned around to check what had now become a digital friend—the red LCD clock. It was 3:01 PM and Mitch wanted to stay the rest of the day at his favorite coffee shop. He looked over at Kayla still lost in her magazine. Suddenly the unmistakable high-pitched tone of a cell phone beeped in rapid succession. Kay had received a text message. Excited, she jumped up to retrieve the message. It must have been good news because she immediately started dialing and soon was engaged in happy conversation. How could a few beeps from a phone initiate such gratification?

Mitch had never sent a text message to anyone, but he had received a few and made it clear to the sender he deplored it. It showed up on his cell phone bill as a charge. "How in the hell can young people afford this?" Mitch would say. Wouldn't it just be easier to pick up the goddamn phone and talk? Perhaps it was a generational thing. After all, *texting* does sound sexy. Mitch remembered when he got his first cell phone. He felt special. Before long, everyone had cell phones and they no longer had their original luster.

Mitch also had an earring a long time ago. This was before most people had one. It was gold and small, but got everyone's attention. Not from the ladies, but from punks accusing Mitch of being gay. It was amazing how many fights a tiny piece of jewelry can cause. It was an old girlfriend's idea. She even pushed the needle through his ear—*that hurt!*

She wanted him to get a tattoo of her name on his right arm, *Lisa*. When Mitch refused she went away and so did the earring. Now, some twenty-five years later it seemed earrings were a status symbol worn by far too many pretentious people trying to impress everyone. To Mitch, tattoos were the same way: Besides, how many people want to see a middle-aged man with a gold earring and a huge Guns N' Roses tattoo?–*Not very sexy*. Mitch's father once told him the only people who have tattoos are sailors or on death row. There are a lot of *both* walking the streets of Seattle.

A cell phone ring filled the coffee shop. Mitch looked around to see some people do the same thing with the same ring tone; reach frantically for their pockets before, god forbid, it would go into voice mail. An expressionless Mr. Wolf reached deep into his inner vest pocket and pulled out a thin-red, sleek cell phone. It was a flip-phone, but he instead of flipping it open, he gently *pulled* it open and calmly said "Hello."

Not only was the old man one of the few in the coffee shop to remain calm while his phone was ringing, he seemed to have no interest in answering it. The person calling must've known the old man very well, and was aware of his deliberate habits.

Mr. Wolf answered: "Oh hello, Dear ..." Mitch could hear inaudible mumbling from what he assumed was Mr. Wolf's wife.

"Oh no, I'm just here at the coffee shop talking to a nice young man. I shouldn't be long. Thank you so much for calling my dear, bye-bye now."

Mr. Wolf closed the phone with the same methodical ease in which he opened it and slid it back into his vest pocket.

"That was my wife; poor dear is worried about me. She always worries, even if I'm just a few minutes late. I should've called and not let the poor old gal sit and worry. I must have lost track of time. She needs me there to take care of her."

A flash went through Mitch's brain. Those words hit close to home. Something his father said some time ago, not long before he died. Mitch called Dad to wish him happy birthday. He called late because he was busy that day. Dad sounded tired and upset.

"Happy birthday, Dad, sorry to call so late."

"It's okay son, I understand. Say I received your card today and I just want to say thank you."

"That's great; I hoped you would get it today. Are you okay Dad? You sound kinda down."

"I'm fine, son, your mother is sick and I'm just here taking care of her."

A long silent pause absorbed the emotion traveling from father to son over the phone line. Mitch held back his tears—hoping Dad wouldn't notice how choked up he was. 'I'm just here taking care of her,' kept repeating in his brain. Not knowing what else to say Mitch said what he always did just before he hung up. Only this time he added something.

"I love you, Dad; you're good man and make sure you tell Mom I love her too. Happy birthday, Dad."

"Thanks, son, love you." It was the last time Mitch said 'Happy birthday Dad.' Dad died six months later.

"Maybe you should go home and see your wife. I'd hate to think she is alone worrying about you because of me," Mitch said.

"That's very considerate of you young man, but the old girl will be fine. She just wanted to hear my voice. It calms her down."

"Yes, it's soothing; it is calming *me* down right now."

"I'll bet you're wondering why I'm sitting here in front of you young man."

"Just call me Mitch if you don't mind. And I'm not that young."

"Oh yes I keep forgetting, Mitch it is then." The old man propped up in the chair as though he was ready to say something important.

IT WAS LATE afternoon at the coffee shop. If this was a regular year it would've been March 1st. But this was a leap year and the February 29th sun started to hang low on the horizon. All the elaborate objects in Mitch's favorite coffee shop were illuminated. The tiny rectangular stained-glass windows above other clear windows were alive with a spectrum of colors. It reminded Mitch when he was a kid in the morning hours attending Catholic Mass. Whenever the priest would give a long sermon Mitch's mind wandered. He'd look up at the beautiful stained-glass images of the Virgin Mary and stages of the cross. Somehow, the morning sun penetrating through those windows said more than a scripted sermon from an old priest.

"I used to be a soldier," the old man said with a somber look. "It was a long time ago when the entire world was at war." *The entire world*, Mitch thought. He didn't say World War II, he said, *the entire world*

153

was at war. Mitch had only heard it a few times in his life. He knew what it meant—a lot of men died.

"I grew up in Liverpool, England," the old man continued.

"Where The Beatles come from," Mitch interjected.

"The who?" Mr. Wolf said looking confused.

"No, not The Who, The Beatles—you know John, Paul, George and Ringo—the band."

"Yes of course, never cared for them. I was conscripted into the Army before any of those chaps were born." A look of pride exuded from the old man's face. It was almost as if he was saying *he* had purpose. After all, when Great Britain and France declared war on Germany September 3, 1939; John, Paul, George and Ringo indeed hadn't been born yet. The old man's face changed when he talked about the war. He looked tired and worn out. Maybe this wasn't a good idea Mitch thought. He could see the horrors of battle on the old man's face. Mitch was about to change the subject when the old man began to speak.

"I don't have much time young man so I will just tell you a quick story before I have to go home to my wife. My grandfather was Jewish and from Poland. He was a master tailor by trade. At the time Poland was occupied by Russia and my grandfather was conscripted into the Russian army to serve in the Russo-Japanese war. Since he was a skilled tailor he was given the task of making uniforms for Russian officers, in particular the generals. He was given a small space to work, completely unsupervised. One day, he decided to make himself a uniform complete with a General's insignia. He stuffed some old clothes into his shirt and resembled the appearance of a well-fed distinguished General.

"My grandfather also made an oversized General's visor hat that partially covered his face. He was only thirty-two so he had to create the illusion of an older man."

Mitch did not want to interrupt but he had to. "How did he do that?"

"I understand your skepticism Mitch. You must understand my grandfather was a resourceful man. He took some light-brown shoe polish and carefully applied it to his face. Then he pulled the visor cap far down over his face and proceeded to walk away from his unit. A disguise *so* authentic he was actually saluted during his escape. Eventually a military escort picked him up and drove him to a train station and had no idea they contributed to his getaway. The train took him to Hamburg, Germany where he embarked on a ship to his destination, Liverpool, England."

Mitch's pessimistic side began to reveal itself. How could someone walk away from his own unit without being recognized? It seemed unlikely. Why would the old man lie? Mitch identified with this distinguished old man. He wondered if this was himself in the future telling unbelievable stories. Yet the old man talked about something very real: *War.* There was something else; it was the way the old man described his grandfather. The hand gestures and his distinctive voice, combined with the authentic look etched on Mr. Wolf's face, confirmed to Mitch he was telling the truth.

The only thing Mitch ever served in was the Cub Scouts, and he got kicked out of that. And why wasn't the old man talking about the war he served in? The war of *all* wars. Mitch sensed by talking about his grandfather's war and avoiding World War II, the war he served in, Mr. Wolf avoided the horrors in his mind.

"That's an amazing story, Mr. Wolf. It sounds like your grandfather had guts. I can't believe he walked out of there that way."

The old man stood up and walked over to Mitch and put his left hand on Mitch's right shoulder and said, "I'm standing in front of you with my hand on your shoulder young man, do you believe me now?"

Mitch looked up like when he was child in front of an unpredictable nun not knowing whether he would be scolded or applauded and said, "I believe you, I'm sorry I doubted you."

"That's quite all right Mitch," as he pulled his hand away and said, "If I were you, I would think the same way."

"I don't mean to pry, but do you have any stories about the war *you* served in you want to share?"

"It was so long ago and I—I can't seem to remember now. Wait, wait there is one. Do you have another minute Mitch my boy?"

"Absolutely," Mitch said as he stretched his arms up high and rested first his left and then his right arm then his palms down on top of the bench seat.

Mr. Wolf sat back down and reached for his paper teacup only to realize it was empty. Mitch asked if he wanted more tea. He declined and looked for a place to put the empty teacup. Mitch reached over, grabbed the cup, got up and walked across the room. The teabag string and paper clasp hanging out from the cup did a trilling dance to the gentle breeze from Mitch's fast-pace-walk. He pushed the lid open and shoved the cup into the garbage can. When he got back the old man looked confused.

"Are you okay, Mr. Wolf?"

"Can you tell me what I was just talking about young man?"

"You were ready to tell me one quick war story but you didn't start yet."

Mr. Wolf looked more confused than ever. He started fumbling through his pockets looking for eyeglasses he was already wearing.

"I don't suppose you've seen my eyeglasses."

"I believe you're wearing them," Mitch said in a calm voice.

"Oh my, I do believe I've lost my good sense."

"Don't worry, you're fine, I can't tell you how many times I've done the same thing."

"You're a gracious and kind man, I'm glad I met you today."

"I feel the same Mr. Wolf. I want you to know I'm

proud of you. You fought against evil and tyranny and lived to tell about it."

"It is to your country and your President Roosevelt that I owe a debt to young man. Without America, we would not have won the war."

Once again as he was with Joe, Mitch was overwhelmed. Something in the way the old man praised America reminded Mitch of his father. In the late afternoon inside Mitch's favorite coffee shop, these strangers, one *not so* young and one old, became friends.

"Oh yes, I recall what I wanted to share with you. May I share it now?"

"Please do." Mitch said with a quick half-smile.

"Right after I turned eighteen, the war started. I was conscripted into the British army. I was told to report to Salisbury Plaines for basic training. Before I left I wanted to visit my grandfather in the hospital because he was very ill. My grandmother had passed away when she was in her early-fifties and I was ten. I loved her dearly and still miss her to this day. She was a kind and loving person. I have fond memories of her. My grandfather remarried, but I did not care for his new wife. I found her to be mean and cold.

"When I visited grandfather or Zweigy, as I sometimes called him, he was alone. He looked weak, nothing like the powerfully built man I knew as a boy. Grandfather was only in his early sixties, but dying of heart disease. They didn't call it that back in those days, just chest pains. My grandfather was nothing like my grandmother. He was difficult to get along with, a perfectionist in every way. Grandfather was always the first one to point out my weaknesses. I hated that. But now, as he lay in the hospital bed he looked peaceful and ready to accept his fate, dressed in a faded white hospital gown with the sheets drawn up to his chest. He spoke in a low raspy tone.

"'Come closer boy I want to tell you something, I wish, I wish I could go with you. I used to be a soldier. Did you hear me? I used to be a soldier.'"

Now, both men played the hospital scene in their minds. The old man had played that scene thousands of times and after today Mitch did the same thing. He would not forget the words: "I used to be a soldier."

"Did you ever see your grandfather again?" Mitch asked.

"No, I went off to boot camp and he died two weeks later. I believe he knew he would die soon, but still wanted me to know if able, he would have come with me. After that night I never remembered him as a man who *used to be a soldier*. I always remembered him *as a soldier*.

"Something strange happened that night in the hospital, young man."

"It's Mitch, remember, but you can call me young man, I kinda like it. What happened in the hospital, Mr. Wolf?"

"You're supposed to call *me* Leo, but now, I like the sound of Mr. Wolf."

Both men laughed as the old man pulled out his

handkerchief and did another trumpet imitation.

"I took a train-ride from Liverpool to the hospital in Leeds where my grandfather spent his final days. On the train ride over I thought of what I would say to him but could not find the words. I was nervous. I was just eighteen and did not know if I would ever come back from the war. You must understand, Mitch; things were scary back then. Hitler built up an enormous fighting force many people thought would trounce over Great Britain. I had a *reason* to be scared. Still, I was ready to fight and show them goddamn Nazis' I wasn't afraid, even though I was petrified.

"The train-ride to the hospital made me drowsy. After I saw my grandfather and heard those haunting words, I was exhausted physically and emotionally. I fell asleep on the chair next to his bed. I was awakened in the night. My frail old dying grandfather had put a blanket over me. I told him to go back to bed and not worry about me." He said, 'I don't want my grandson to be cold.' Somehow he managed to get out of the hospital bed in the night and cover me with a blanket."

"He loved you, Mr. Wolf, I don't know if he ever told you, but after hearing this I'm certain, he loved you."

"He *never* told me he loved me, but I believe you're right."

"He wanted to come with you and if he were young I bet he would have," Mitch said.

"Yes, he would," the old man said sadly from

160

either remembering the last time he saw his grand-father so ill or just missing him. It was so many years ago he wasn't sure anymore.

"Can you help me to my car young man? I must be going. The poor old girl will be worried sick if I stay any longer."

"Certainly, Mr. Wolf, I'm sorry I took so much of your time. Tell your wife it's *my* fault."

"I just might do that Mitch my boy. Here, let me grab my things."

Mr. Wolf put on his overcoat, red scarf and hat in the same methodical manner in which he took them off. Mitch grabbed Mr. Wolf's brown umbrella and took one slow, long step for every two of the old man's. As they approached the front door Kayla gave them both a wide smile.

The rain returned and as soon as Mitch opened the door the loud swooshes of cars and water cascad-ing down from overflowing gutters revealed the Northwest winter was not over. It was cold with a slight breeze. Mitch popped open the umbrella with a slow whipping sound until it opened and locked. He gently put his right hand around the old man's left arm just above the elbow and yelled: "WHERE DID YOU PARK, MR. WOLF?!" It was raining hard now and the noise from passing cars made it hard to hear.

"JUST ACROSS THE STREET, *THERE*, DIRECTLY IN FRONT OF US!" Mr. Wolf said looking confused again. While they waited for traffic to subside, Mitch took one more look at this intriguing fellow. He wondered if he would ever see him again and how much time he had left on earth—how much time did any of us have? Mitch saw an opening and lightly pulled the old man across the street while trying to shield them with his oversized brown umbrella.

When they got to Mr. Wolf's car he quickly opened the door with his key and told Mitch to put the umbrella on the back seat. The old man got in, shut the door and rolled down the window about six inches, just enough to say goodbye and reach his hand out to Mitch one more time. Funny, his hands were soft and warm, just like Mitch's.

"I hope I see you again sometime young man."

"Same here, Mr. Wolf, and thanks for everything."

"Is it safe to back up I can barely see?" Mr. Wolf said unable able to turn around all the way.

"Yeah, come on back, I'll watch the road for you," Mitch said as he motioned his hands like a traffic cop. The old man pulled back and stopped one more time.

"Bye-bye, now young man and God bless you." Before Mitch could reply the old man had pulled into traffic. Mitch thought about those last words, 'God bless you.'

Was this day's peculiar turn of events preordained in God's grand scheme? If it was, where did Mitch fit in the picture? He had no explanation. His presence *was* his purpose.

Mitch watched the old man's car until it faded out of view. A habit he picked up from Mom that somehow stuck with him all these years. He wondered how

Mom was doing and if he should call her. What would he say about the people he met today?

Mitch realized he was standing in the rain day-dreaming. No big deal, it's not as if he was from California where the people would say to him when he had some outdoor carpentry work, "You can't work in this rain today, you'll melt." Mitch's proud response, "It's okay Ma'am, I'm from around here." But this was *hard*, cold Seattle rain and Mitch was getting wet. He ran back across the street and rested under the eaves of the coffee shop with his back to the wall.

Across the street near the entrance to a park he saw an old couple walking a huge chocolate lab that kept chasing after crows. After every unsuccessful attempt to catch a crow, the dog would return to its owners and jump up and down while wagging its tail, as if to say, 'I tried, I tried.' Mitch laughed out loud and walked toward the front door. Something caught his eye at the park entrance just in between two tall, black railed metal gates that were folded open.

FIVE

THE INSTRUMENT

ITCH WAS COLD, WET AND WITHOUT A JACKET, but could not take his eyes off the park entrance. Someone was standing there, right in between the metal gates with a big, dark-red umbrella. It was a girl or perhaps a small woman with the umbrella partially covering her face. Mitch decided to wait outside under the eaves a little longer. The big chocolate lab approached and sat down in front of her. It looked up at her as its tail dragged back and forth on the wet pavement. She made no attempt to pet it. She didn't move. Was she afraid, or was it something else? Mitch wanted to know. He waved not knowing if she could see him. The red umbrella slowly tilted upward. Mitch could see rain drops bounce off it. The rain clouds grew darker.

He went back inside the coffee shop. Kayla was starting to close. It was 4:30 PM and the coffee shop did not close until six. Kayla had plans for the evening. Her boyfriend called and she was in a good mood.

"I can't believe you stayed all day today, Mitch," she said as she wiped down a table.

"I can't believe it either, and I'm still here."

"Might as well stay till I close—I sure appreciate the company," Kayla said as she walked to the next table to wipe down.

"I suppose I could stay a while longer. Hey, throw me a towel so I can help you wipe these tables down."

"Jeez, thanks Mitch," Kayla said excited she had just found a free helper.

They wiped all the tables and Kayla collected three full white plastic trash bags to take out.

"I'll take those for you; it's nasty out there."

"You're the best customer Mitch."

"I know."

Mitch grabbed the plastic bags, intertwined six yellow plastic strings together and threw them over his back. He knew where the dumpster was because he parked across from it out back. Mitch stumbled out the back door, found the dumpster and lifted the lid. The bags tumbled down with the sound of glass striking metal at the bottom of the empty dumpster. The plastic lid slammed back down and Mitch walked to the coffee shop, indifferent to the weather. The rain had let up little, but not enough to keep him from becoming wetter. When he got back inside he saw a trail of water from the front door all the way to the bottom of the spiral staircase.

"Did someone go up there?" Mitch asked Kayla.

"Yes, I saw an Asian girl with a red umbrella. She came in right after you went out back. She tried to shake off the water outside. She didn't say anything, but walked up the stairs. Mitch, I think something is wrong. I saw her face, I *know* something's wrong."

Mitch didn't bother to ask more. He sensed it from across the street. He knew what he had to do. He walked to the spiral staircase.

"Whatta ya gonna do, Mitch?" Kayla said and then nervously bit her bottom lip.

"I'm going up there."

This was the essence of Mitch Lucas the man—not knowing *what* he would do and yet trusting he would do the right thing. Just walk up the stairs and confront a total stranger, unsure and unafraid of the outcome. He had to do it. Why, was not important. He looked at the red LCD clock—4:51 PM.

He ascended the steps and thought of what he might say. The more he thought the more he wanted go back down. He stopped worrying near the top. The door was open half way with a few sprinkles of water on the floor. Mitch stood there for a moment, took a few deep breaths and walked inside.

He looked to the left at the plastic table and then to the narrow wooden bench seat. They were empty. "Where did she go?" he wondered. Then, he saw the red umbrella hanging on the narrow window ledge. She stood next to it at a slight angle looking out the window and down. Again, Mitch could not see her

167

face clearly. He said nothing and hoped she would look over. She did not. Mitch walked toward the wooden bench and the girl abruptly turned, accidentally knocking the folded red umbrella on the floor. They both bent down to pick it up, but grabbed it at the same time. Mitch's big hand held the hook shaped wooden handle while her small hand held the narrow silver tip. Their heads tilted up in unison until they locked in a gaze.

Now Mitch could see what he missed before. There was no mistaking it, not with his face so close to hers. He could tell she had cried. Kayla was right, something was indeed wrong. They stayed in the same position, looked at each other and wondered what to do next. Finally, she slowly stood up as she let go of the umbrella. Mitch followed and hung it back on the windowsill. "Thank you, you're so kind," she said.

"No problem, by the way my name is Mitch; it's nice to meet you."

"My name is Michelle, nice to meet you, too, Sir."

"You can call me *anything* but sir," Mitch said cracking a smile. Michelle smiled back and Mitch was happy.

Michelle had medium length, straight black hair and dark-brown eyes. Mitch might not have noticed the color of her eyes on another day, but today they were sad. He was mesmerized by them. She was around five-feet-tall, but it was hard to tell with her hunched over. Mitch thought the brown leather boots that were laced six inches above her ankles gave an illusion, making her taller. Then, he saw very little heel. When she did stand up straight, her true height was revealed.

Even though she used an umbrella, the ends of her hair were wet. An occasional drop of water would fall and bead up on the shiny floor. She stood only three feet away from Mitch, yet had no idea just how *close* he was to her. Not in the physical sense, but in the undefined wavelength that draws two strangers together. She felt calm and wanted to stay. Why, she thought, why did she feel this way? It didn't matter. Just to be there with this kind man was enough.

Mitch felt the same way as he did when he first met Sarah. *Almost,* except for the aura that exuded from this stranger with dark-brown eyes was overpowering. Mitch had difficulty absorbing it. And there was something else, something about the dark-red umbrella. When Mitch touched it his mind flashed and he sensed suffering: though the instrument designed to shield against the rain had somehow absorbed the suffering this woman had in her heart.

Mitch asked if she wanted to go downstairs and grab a table. "I'll buy you a coffee."

"No, no, you don't need to do that," she said avoiding eye contact.

"It's okay, I want to," as he reached for the umbrella and they descended the spiral staircase. He began to lose track of how many times he had been up and down these steps today. Was it the last time— maybe ever?

When they reached the bottom Kayla smiled and winked at Mitch. Mitch returned the gesture and escorted his new friend to a table by the front door. It was late, 5:15 now and the coffee shop would close soon. Kayla cleaned up the day's slop with her head bobbing back and forth to the music blaring through the tiny white speakers of her iPod.

Once again the rain stopped and clouds were on the move. A mixed-bag day: wind, showers followed by hard rain and light hail—intermixed with stints of sunshine. A blend of weather unique to Seattle. The girl with dark-brown eyes carefully hung her umbrella on the chair by the table behind them and sat down. They were at the round small table closest to the front door where outside Mitch had spotted her. It seemed like a long time ago.

"I really don't want coffee. It's kind of late for it, don't you think?"

"It's never too late for coffee, but I do believe I've had enough today."

"Did you see me look at you when you were over at the entrance to the park?" Mitch asked.

"I don't know. I was just standing there listening to the rain on my umbrella."

"Did you see that dog?" Mitch asked.

"Yes, but I don't like big dogs, I'm very afraid."

"I understand, but that dog liked you. Couldn't you see its tail wagging?"

"What does it mean? Tail wagging."

"It means the dog likes you, silly, can't you see my tail wagging now?"

She covered her mouth, started giggling and Mitch joined in. For a moment the sadness on her face subsided, but shortly after the laughter stopped it returned. Mitch could see it in her eyes, but was afraid to ask.

The sun had found its way out and now rested just above a band of dark-grey clouds. It would soon set and Mitch, once again, was glad he picked this day to spend at the coffee shop. He was curious, but did not want to make her feel uncomfortable with questions. Michelle finally spoke. "Do you like here, at this coffee shop?"

"Yes, very much, why do you ask?"

"You look at peace here."

"I like it here, but it's the first time I've been here on a Sunday."

Michelle leaned over the table so her face was closer. "Your eyes are dark-brown, did you know that?"

"No, I always thought they were black"—she quickly dug in her purse to find a mirror to see if Mitch was teasing. Her small mouth opened wide and then her eyes, as she discovered her eyes were indeed dark-brown.

"I can't believe it, I myself never noticed. It seems you knew I didn't know."

"I didn't know for sure, but you'd be surprised

how many people don't know the true color of their eyes. You look Chinese and most Chinese people have black eyes. Are you from China?"

"Yes, from Beijing," she said brushing the bangs of hair away from her eyes to reveal what Mitch had already discovered. "I have been in Seattle almost ten years and I'm very homesick now." Her eyes were now glossed with tears waiting to drench an unfair world and reveal one more lonely soul.

Mitch struck a chord of sadness by asking where she was from. He thought he was making things worse and waited for Michelle to speak.

The red LCD digital clock that now felt like an old friend read 5:39 PM and Kayla told Mitch they could stay until she finished cleaning up. Mitch and Michelle shared their first uncomfortable moment together in silence. Michelle composed herself and talked about her family. "Sometimes I want to go back to China, but then I remember how hard my life was there. Now I need—I *need* to go back home."

"Do you mind if I ask why," Mitch asked.

"I don't mind, but I'm scared to tell anyone. I'm so afraid right now."

A moment passed. Not knowing what to do Mitch moved his long-fingered hand over Michelle's resting on the table and said, "I'm afraid too, almost every day."

"Why is this first time you come here on Sunday?"

"My mother is sick and she didn't want me to visit her which I usually do on Sundays. I don't care if I get sick but she does—I mean after all it's just a cold.

She sounded so tired and weak I decided to leave her alone to rest."

"Is she okay, other than the cold I mean to say?"

"Not really."

"What do you mean 'not really,' what is wrong with your mother?" Michelle asked with urgency.

"She has emphysema."

"What is emphfaazzma?"

"She smoked most of her life and now she can barely breathe. She has to use a machine to help her breathe."

Michelle looked away and out the window. It seemed to Mitch she was looking at the entrance to the park—the spot where he first saw her. It was 5:50 PM—almost closing time. Kayla was almost done with clean-up. Mitch wondered what to do next. Michelle quickly turned her glance from the park and looked Mitch in the face. She looked upset. Her intense glare intimidated him, but he did not turn away and sat there looking into her dark-brown eyes. Then, Michelle asked him a strange question. "Do you love your mother?"

"More than *anything* in this world. I would do anything for my mother and will not tolerate anyone talking bad about her. I suppose I'm a lot like her, very stubborn and unwilling to give in to what I feel is right. I think my mom would like you Michelle."

"How do you know your mother would like me?"

"Because you both see through the bullshit in life, to what's real and matters."

"How do you know I can do that?"

Smiling now Mitch asked, "Can you?"

"Yes, I can, I am just wondering how you knew?"

"Don't wonder, just accept it."

"You should go visit your mother, I think she needs you."

"I told you, I would, but she is sick today and didn't want me to get sick."

"But *you* want to visit her, don't you?" Michelle said as she propped up in the chair.

"I do, but sometimes it's so hard seeing her and knowing she's dying. It's like I am *dying* with her. There is nothing I can do except watch and hope I can keep her here, alive. Yet, there is another part of me that just hates to see her suffer. So you see I feel tormented either way.

"When I visit, she's always happy to see me and that makes me happy. After a while I can see the grief in her face: The sadness of missing my father and living alone. I wish I could give her my health and strength, but I cannot. All I can do is be there for her and believe me, as long as life is in me, I will."

"Do you always talk this way?"

"No, why?"

"I don't know why I ask, you seem so different."

"So do you, Michelle."

Kayla gathered the remaining trash from the kitchen into one huge black garbage bag. She looked over at Mitch and gave him that ... 'Could you please take this out for me look?' without hesitation he offered, "Let me get that for you, darling."

"I'll be right back; will you please wait for me?"

"No ..."

For a brief moment, Mitch was hurt, almost as if someone stuck a knife in his back—until Michelle said, "I would like you to walk me home if you don't mind. I want to talk to you some more. Please walk with me—I don't live far away."

Mitch grabbed the black garbage bag Kayla had put near the back door and told Kayla he was going to walk his new friend home.

"Have fun you two," she said as Mitch fumbled with the trash bag. Michelle picked up her coat and dark-red umbrella. They headed for the back door and Mitch bid farewell to his favorite barista. Kayla's cell phone rang again and the last impression in Mitch's mind was a big smile as she wiped off the espresso machine with her cell phone propped in between her right cheek and shoulder—talking the talk only young lovers understand.

She gave Mitch one last wave and smile as he and Michelle rushed out the back door into the alleyway. The *old friend* red LCD clock read 6:00 PM exactly. The coffee shop was closed.

Mitch opened the dumpster lid, took a few steps back, and heaved the garbage bag with the expertise of a discus thrower. He did two quick revolutions with the yellow twist ties in his right hand and hurled the bag up and into the dark-blue dumpster.

"Do you do that every time?" Michelle asked.

"Not *every* time, it's just something I picked up from my older brother Paul, a long time ago and I've been doing ever since."

"You're really good at it."

"I should be. I've done it for thirty years now."

"Will you walk me home now?"

"I would be happy to."

SIX

PINK RHODODENDRON

THE RAIN STOPPED AND SKY WAS CLEAR. THE SUN was down and early evening twilight illuminated the grey pavement still wet from the rain. It was the last day of February in a leap year. On three out of the four other years it would have been the 1st of March. Not this year. This was the one year in every four which most calendars read the peculiar date: February 29th.

They walked down the alleyway, through the parking lot and passed by Mitch's truck. Michelle instinctively opened her dark-red umbrella. She pressed the silver metal clip with her black leather gloved hands. It slowly opened with the grinding metal on metal sound and locked open. Mitch realized there was no need for the umbrella. "I don't think you'll need that, it's clearing up."

"I'm just so used to the rain. I open my umbrella without thinking. I think it's raining, or will be soon."

"And most of time you'd be right, but now I don't think you need that beautiful umbrella. By the way, where did you get it?"

"My mother gave it to me for my tenth birthday. It was way too big for me then. She said I would grow in to it. I used to walk around in the rain twirling this umbrella and jump into puddles with my yellow boots. Sometimes I would hold it in front of me and my mother would say the only thing you could see coming down the street was a huge red umbrella and tiny yellow boots."

Mitch could picture a little ten-year-old Chinese girl walking down the street in the rain with a red umbrella almost as big as she, stomping in puddles—having fun without worrying about getting wet or catching cold. Just being a little girl with her big umbrella. This thought made him smile until Michelle interrupted Mitch's daydream by saying: "Please walk me home now, I don't like to walk in the dark."

"How far is it to your home?"

"I'm not very good with measurements—perhaps a mile or less."

"I'll have you home before it gets dark and even if it does, don't worry; I'll take care of you—I promise."

"I can't believe I'm letting you walk me home. You're still a stranger. Usually I must build up the trust before I do something like this. Somehow I feel I know you. Does that sound strange?"

"After today and the people I've met, nothing sounds strange. All I know is we're here, *right now*, for a reason. What that reason is, I do not know. If you don't feel comfortable with me just say so and I'll walk away. I would rather do that than make you uncomfortable."

"No, no, I didn't mean it that way—I want you to walk me home. Please come with me now."

Mitch and Michelle walked to the busy street corner adjacent to the coffee shop. The cars and trucks roared by. They had their headlights on and illuminated the wet pavement. The sun had set at 5:53 PM. on this last day of February in this rare leap year. It was just after six o'clock and the early evening twilight hinted the coming of spring. This was Mitch's favorite time of year and day. His light-sensitive hazel-eyes could see in this light better than at any other time of day. Dad's birthday was on January 4th. He always called Dad to tell him how happy he was that the days were getting longer. Dad was always glad to hear from his son.

"Which way is home, red umbrella girl?"

Michelle pointed toward the park entrance where Mitch first saw her. "That way, I live on the other side of the park." The park was kitty-corner from the coffee shop. Instead of waiting for the bright white silhouetted walkman, Mitch waited until the traffic was clear, grabbed Michelle's arm and pulled her to the park entrance corner. The whole time Michelle complained it was *against* the law to do this.

"I break the law every day. *Don't worry*; I'm not talking about the serious laws like murder or robbing a bank. I'm talking about silly laws like spitting on the sidewalk or walking across the street, or not having a garbage bag in your car."

"Really, is there such a law?" Michelle said in bewilderment.

"In this state there is. But that's Washington for you. They invent laws to make money, even though they can't enforce them."

"It's stupid to have such a law. Do you have a trash bag in your truck?"

"Yes, I do, but not because I have to. I have one because I hate to litter. It was something my dad taught me when I was young. He always had a trash bag in the car. Not because it was a law, it wasn't back then. He was just very clean and organized."

"Do you have a trash bag in *your* car?" Mitch said teasingly.

"No, I don't, I just throw the trash on the floor and pick it up whenever I can. Maybe I should get a trash bag before I get pulled over and they put me in the jail."

"See, you break the law too, and you didn't even know it—everybody does, even the people who create the very same laws." They laughed about absurd laws meant to be broken as they walked toward the tall black metal gates where Mitch first saw her.

When they walked past the gates he looked over at Michelle and said: "I will not forget the first time I saw you standing here with that beautiful red umbrella. I must admit, when I first saw you I sensed something was wrong. Is there something wrong?" Michelle looked down, "I just found out my mom died. My sister called me from Beijing and told me. I was in my car and my sister held up the phone to the machine that monitors her heartbeat and it stopped—we both heard it stop, but I was so far away. What do you call it when those machines just stop? What is the word?"

"Flatline," Mitch said as Michelle stopped walking. "Yes, *flatline*. That's what it sounded like. Her heart was beating very quickly, then *very* slowly—then … just a loud tone, a flat line as you say."

They stood by the tall black metal gates and entrance to the park. Mitch could see a light on in the kitchen of the coffee shop. The light turned off and Kayla came out the front door and locked it. She walked across a parking lot still chatting on her cell phone, got in her tiny silver Prius and drove away. The car made almost no noise at all—just tires swooshing across wet pavement.

Mitch stood beside this woman who had just found out her Mother died. What could he do or *say* to take away her sorrow and grief? He thought of his own Mother and how much he missed her. What would he do when she died? What could he do? And why was this happening to him? All these strange stories—heroic, horrific and sad stories on the same day—could *any* of this be real? They were real stories from real people. Mitch realized once again, what he needed to do.

"I'm sorry Michelle. I can't imagine losing my mother. When my father died suddenly of a heart attack it didn't seem fair. I spoke with him just ten days before he died."

"What did you talk about?"

"It was Father's Day, and I called him as I did every Father's Day. Except this time would be the last time. He was having problems with his legs—some blood circulation problem. I knew he had health problems, but I figured the doctors would fix him. His father, my grandfather, died of a heart attack when he was only thirty-nine. My dad was just fifteen and I remember he said I was lucky to have him around. He's right, I was.

"The grandfather I never met got up one day, ate breakfast, and walked to work. While he walked across a bridge he fell down and died. The funny thing is, he had a car and drove across the very same bridge every day to work. Out of nowhere he decided to walk to work that day. He told my grandmother he didn't get enough exercise, so he was going to walk each day. Well, it turned out to be only *one* day. And not even that, if you think about it, because he died on the middle of the bridge in the early morning hours on a bright, sunny spring day. He didn't even make it across the bridge."

"And your dad, what did you say to your dad the last time you talked with him?"

"Mostly small stuff, you know *guy* stuff. But something was strange in the way he spoke to me."

"What you mean?"

"Well, he told me he wanted to get together with me and my mother."

"I don't think it's strange; he probably missed you."

"Yes, I'm sure he did but when he said, 'Son we need to get together, and son, better make it soon.'"

Michelle's eyes opened wide. "Did he say it to you like that?"

"Yes he did. Then I knew something was wrong. But I put it out of my mind. That was until ten days later when I got a message on my cell phone from my mother: 'Mitchell,' that's what my mother always calls me, 'call home, now.' I already knew by the sound of my mother's voice that my father was dead."

"How did you know?"

"By the weak frailty of my mother's voice—in her voice I could hear that my dad's life was over. It was a strange day in late June. The beginning of summer, but it was a cool, gray day. I had made plans to meet a customer that day to give her a bid on carpentry work. Then I listened to the message Mom left on my cell phone."

"What did you do? Did you call your customer?"

"No, I just showed up like nothing happened. This is a commercial job I had done for about two years. It's a husband and wife business—something to do with computer repair. They do very well, I still have the job. Anyway, the building they own is old and rundown so once in a while I do some repair work. On the day Dad died I arranged to meet Margaret, my customer, at the office. Her husband William wasn't around so she showed me the repair work she wanted done around the base of the building."

"What kind of repair work?"

"Oh, just some basic dry rot removal and replacement. You can't just half-ass it, because it has to be done up to code. Anyway, she's a sweet old-lady and always kind and polite. I remember walking around the building, *wanting* to tell her I just found out my father died."

"Did you—did you tell her?"

"I *wanted* to, but did not want to ruin her day, so we just walked around and I pretended to pay attention while trying not to cry. And you wanna know something funny?"

"What could be funny about your father dying?"

"Nothing, it's just I don't think she knew anything was wrong. Somehow the cool breeze on that gray, early-summer day took away my sorrow—just for a moment."

Michelle started to walk slowly. Mitch did his best not to shoot out in front of her. It was always hard for him to walk this slowly. Now it seemed easy as he did something he had not done in a long time. *Take his time*. It didn't matter, nothing seemed to matter anymore. Each methodic step with this woman, this stranger, and yet someone he had always known, erased all pain from the past.

The emptiness he had carried around from deep inside himself was gone. He didn't know where it went. Mitch had changed more this day than any other. The change was good. His past was in steps behind and life's answers in the steps ahead. They walked the path together as the almost full moon crept up the hillside in luminescent wonder.

The park trail wasn't really a trail at all. It was dark-gray paved asphalt with an old weathered look from years of people walking, riding their bikes, and pounding their running shoes on it. This trail was in the middle of two grass hills that meandered up slopes that led up to an apartment or condominium. Bark beds filled both sides of the trail with signs of spring. Tulips and daffodils pushed up just enough to expose their buds.

Even though it was February 29th, this was the Pacific Northwest, and that meant on a clear night, such as tonight, it would get cold. Might even freeze, Mitch thought. Both hillsides featured neatly carved out circles around beautiful white dogwood trees. The evening twilight combined with the rising moonlight illuminated the early white blossoms.

"Look at those trees," Michelle said, "they're so beautiful."

"Yes, they look like giant pearls in the air," Mitch said looking up.

"Yes, giant white beautiful pearls."

February is the month the Northwest gains the most daylight hours. Each leap year, February features the addition of one extra day and three extra minutes of precious daylight. But the twilight was

LEAP YEAR AT THE COFFEE SHOP

fading and night would soon dispose of the day.

"My apartment is over there. We're not too far now. I want to thank you so much for walking me home and listening. Today is a sad day for me. I don't know how to explain. English is not my native language. I wish I could ..."

"No need to explain, I understand—believe me I do. And you speak English very well."

"Thank you, I almost forgot to say—today's my dad's birthday. Actually, it was yesterday because Beijing is about sixteen hours ahead of our time. Every leap year I celebrate my dad's birthday on February 29th, Seattle time. I feel more connected to him that way."

"So your mother died on your *dad's* birthday?"

"No, because it is March 1st in Beijing already, so we usually celebrate my dad's birthday that day. This means I have to call him the day before and wish him, 'Happy Birthday.' Yesterday when I called him it was truly his birthday, February 29th. Usually, I call the evening of February 28th. Of course it is the same now except it is a leap year.

"My mother died today at four-thirty in the p.m. our time. It was ten-thirty in the a.m. Beijing time. Right now it is already Monday in Beijing. I was sitting in my car talking with my sister when I heard the flatline as you say. *I heard my mother die:* Over the phone from across the world. I told my sister I would talk later. I could not speak. Then I sat in my car for a while, got out and grabbed my umbrella from the trunk and started walking. I didn't know I was walking by the entrance to the park until I stopped and saw that dog looking at me with its tail wagging. It started to rain hard and I knew for sure my mother was dead."

"I'm so sorry, Michelle. Does your dad know about your mother? Have you or your sister told him yet?"

"No, we have not. I don't think he would know if we did tell him. You see my father has Alzheimer's and I don't know if he would understand."

"Is he staying near your mother?"

"They were in same hospital—in same room. My mother was dying of kidney failure so they kept moving her into intensive care and then back with my father until they moved her back into intensive care for good. Then, I sensed something was wrong so I called my sister. That's when I heard her die. I don't know if my dad knows what's going on. I don't know how to tell him. I don't know if he would understand. My sister says he doesn't even recognize his grandson, my sister's only son."

"Is that his only grandchild?"

"Yes, and I don't think if my dad knows who he is."

Mitch stood about five feet in front of Michelle with his back to her. He heard the umbrella open, turned around and saw just a slight hue of dark red with silver tips illuminated from the moon, shielding Michelle's face. Then he heard crying covered by a dark silhouetted device meant for shielding against the rain. But *the rain*—the crying came from under the shield. The sky was a dark-grayish blue and a few stars that could not wait for night, shown their brilliance. Michelle succumbed to the unmistakable, unforgettable sorrow of losing her mother. This was unbearable for Mitch to watch. The end of a parent's life creates the realization of one's own mortality.

Mitch sensed this right after his dad died. And what about Mom—how much time did she have left? The emphysema brought on by decades of smoking took its toll. The thought of losing his mother and watching Michelle right after losing hers was too much. Mitch cried. It was funny; he could not remember the last time he cried. Michelle overheard some sniffling and slowly lifted the umbrella until she saw Mitch with his back to her and head down—she had never seen a strong man, someone full of confidence and vitality diminished to weeping openly.

The moonlight illuminated the trail *just enough* for Mitch to see. The moon, *just seeing it*, always had a profound effect on his emotions. It stirred from deep within the ancient wonder of its relationship with Earth. To Mitch, the moon and earth were friends, pushing and pulling in perpetual alliance.

The moon was witnessing a sad moment between strangers brought together under its pale light. A perfect setting for sharing and understanding the need— the undeniable *need* to have someone there to talk to and listen.

As Mitch composed himself, Michelle walked around him as she closed the umbrella. Mitch's watering eyes did not want to look at hers. He was embarrassed and looked down at her boots. Then, he looked up and saw a small hand reach out, bathed by the moonlight. She grabbed his strong right hand and said, "It's okay to cry." Their hands touched as their eyes met. Two sets of eyes mirrored each other's deepest sorrow by looking into each other's soul. Time stood still.

Michelle moved closer and gently put her ear on Mitch's chest. She reached her arms around him and could hear and feel his loud heartbeat. Mitch ran his fingers through her silky black hair and dropped his arms over her shoulders. They held each other as though their very existence depended on it—no words were spoken, none were needed.

Mitch rested his chin on Michelle's head as she looked over and saw her apartment building. The lights around the building bid 'welcome home' against a backdrop of deep, dark-blue sky. It was seconds away from nightfall on this last day of February in a leap year. "Please take me home now."

"Okay, just let me hold you a little longer...."

THEY WALKED DOWN the path that ended in front of the apartment building. Michelle held Mitch's hand: A sign of trust? Or a sign she felt comfortable with this unusual man. Usually by now some early blooming rhododendrons would show signs of life. But this had been a cold winter with abundant snow and the early bloomers were still hiding. "My apartment is right over there, I can walk from here."

"I'll walk you over, it's no problem, I want to."

"Okay, but I cannot invite you in. It's not that I don't trust you, I do. You must believe me. It's just that I *need* to be alone right now."

"You don't have to explain anything to me. I understand. What will you do now? Will you go back home? Can you make it back home?"

"I don't know. It's so far away and I can't think of, how, *or if* I can get back home."

I can't think of, how, or if I can get back home. What did that mean? Did it mean she was afraid? To travel thousands of miles only to be confronted with the crushing reality her mother was dead. Or, maybe she had just started a new job and could not take time off. She *just* found out her mother died. Michelle was in shock. Mitch realized this the first moment he saw her standing in the rain in front of the big black metal gates with her red umbrella. He wondered if all people who just lost a parent or loved one, exuded an aura of sorrow only others who had lost could understand. Now, he realized how he might have looked to strangers when his father died—*the look* of desperation, loneliness and disbelief: *The look* of no longer having someone, who meant *everything*—gone into nothingness.

Michelle said it was time to go in. Mitch offered to walk her to the door. She insisted on going alone. In her depressed state she could not see the disappointment in Mitch's eyes. It was time to go, but he wasn't *ready* to say goodbye. As they waited in front of her apartment in an uncomfortable moment when strangers must part not knowing if they will ever see each other again, a light turned on outside. It must've been on a timer and not a sensor because it was already dark. The light shone over a beautiful pink rhododendron in full bloom. The entire row was illuminated, but only one rhododendron bloomed, the one directly below the bright light. Mitch was ready to offer this was a sign of hope and rebirth but instead remained silent. Michelle looked at the pink rhododendron and smiled. "It's beautiful. I love that color."

"Yes, it's very pretty."

"Thank you for walking me home, I will not forget you."

"I don't know *how* I could ever forget you. I've never met anyone like you. And I'm so sorry about your mother."

"Thank you, Mitch, I must now go. Goodbye."

They hugged one last time. *Was* it the last time—how could they know? Whatever was in Michelle's heart was hers. Something sacred—something *no one* could touch. Not even Mitch, the man who believed he could reach anyone. All that meant nothing now.

He looked into Michelle's eyes one last time, smiled, and turned to walk away. He took a few steps and heard her boots clanking on the stairs as she walked down to what must have been a lower-level apartment. Mitch also heard the sound of metal hit pavement. She was walking the red umbrella down the stairs. The noise stopped and Mitch turned and looked back one more time, but only saw the pink blossoming rhododendron under the artificial white light. Michelle was gone.

MITCH WALKED BACK to the coffee shop with his usual gait. A brisk pace, the way he always walked. It was strange, he felt Michelle beside him. He would feel her presence beside him, especially when he was *alone*. He did not see her again, but thought of her. Somehow, he knew she would be okay. In his darkest moments Michelle's spirit soothed his lonely, troubled soul and brought him peace. The relationship that never was, was the romance of his life. A gift he cherished for the rest of his life.

SEVEN

I HAD TO SEE YOU

B EFORE HE REALIZED WHERE HE WAS, MITCH looked up and the coffee shop was in front of him. It looked dead. Like an old house with no lights on and no one home. No people, no stories and no one to tell him what had just happened.

Never again did he look at anyone the way he did before this day at the coffee shop. For the first time, Mitch realized people needed him and in his own unique way, *he* needed them. No longer a man isolated on an island of indifference. But a man who belonged—just like when he was a little boy on Saint Luke's playground.

His clean black truck reflected moonlight in the darkest corner of the parking lot. A spot reserved, at least in Mitch's mind, for him. One push of the key remote and his truck lights reflected off the parking lot wall saying, "welcome back." He hurried into the truck, shut the door and turned off the lights. He preferred the dark. Mitch loved the day and sunlight, but night blanketed his loneliness and helped forget the pain in his heart. Now, after Michelle he had no need to wallow in the dark. The pain was *gone*.

He started his truck and let it warm up. The muffled idol of its powerful V8 engine slowly heated. Mitch waited a few minutes and then turned on the dashboard heat. He rubbed his hands quickly together as they warmed. "What happened today?" he thought sitting in his truck and looking up at the moon. He could've sat there all night pondering what caused him to be different. Could a man change that much in one day? Mitch did—and he couldn't figure out why. In time, he no longer felt the need to try.

He remembered what his father said about acquiring only a few "true friends" in one's whole life. Even though Mitch would not see the people he had met this day again, he would think of them as friends. *Dad was wrong*. Friendship is not about a long commitment. It is about being there for someone and listening when they *need* it. In his heart, he hoped *he* would be remembered by the people he met on this February 29th as a friend. Someone who listened and cared....

Finally, he backed-up his truck and pulled out. Turn left and its five minutes to home. He could not go home—not now. He took a right and started driving—destination unknown. He ended up on the freeway heading south toward Mom's apartment. *"Don't come visit me today, son, I don't want to get you sick,"* kept going through his mind. "Ah the hell with it, I want to see her, NOW!" First he had to stop and pick up some fish and chowder for dinner. Mom was picky; she liked her clam chowder piping hot. Mitch figured if he showed up at the front door with dinner, Mom just might forget what she said earlier. At least that was the plan....

He stood at Mom's front door with the hot bag of goodies in one hand and a cold pop in the other. He put the pop on the ground and knocked loudly. Mom was hooked up to an oxygen machine and sometimes could not hear him knock.

"Who is it?"

"It's your son."

"Just a minute."

Mitch waited in quiet apprehension, wondering what Mom's reaction would be. "Come in Mitchell, the door is open." Mitch didn't understand why she never locked the door. Every time he showed up it was open, even now when he was unexpected. Did she *ever* lock that door? She said she would lock it before she went to bed and Mitch wanted to stop by at three in the morning to see if it was still open. Mom was stubborn and did things her way.

Mitch opened the door and walked into the living room. He saw Mom sitting in her favorite chair. She smiled. "I can see you brought food Mitchell."

"It's your favorite Mom, cod-fish and hot chowder."

"Are you sure the chowder's hot? Maybe you should heat it up in the microwave."

"Just try it Mom and if it's not hot enough I will take care of it for you."

"You're a good son Mitchell, I'm glad you brought me dinner, I'm so hungry."

"I'll get it ready Mom and after that I'll get right to work cleaning this place up."

"I know you will, but don't worry about that now. Let's eat." Mom's voice had a stuffed up tone to go with her red nose that she had blown many times. Mitch didn't say a word about her cold. Nor did he care if he got sick. Mom always took care of him when he was sick.

Mitch walked back out the front door to pick up his pop. As he bent down, he looked over and noticed the moon reflecting off the river—the swirling water next to a log gave the mirrored moon an illusion it was spinning. Mom lived close to a beautiful river and Mitch would often walk down to its banks to relax and reminisce. "Why is the moon so bright?" he thought to himself. The moon on this last day of February in a leap year had seen him change more than any other. The black was now bright. He went back inside and enjoyed dinner with his mother.

"Sorry Mom, I just *had* to see you tonight."

"It's okay, Mitchell, I love you."

"I love you too, Mom."

.....

MITCH'S MOTHER DIED five days later. The emphysema that had robbed her body of oxygen for so many years finally took her life. Mitch never got the chance to tell her what happened that Sunday at the coffee shop. Only Mom or perhaps Dad would understand. They were *both* gone now.

Right before Mom died, Mitch hesitated to visit her at the hospital. He did not want to accept the inevitable. Everyone had been there to say goodbye, except him. When he arrived she was unconscious— her heart beating fast. She was hooked-up to some machine. Mitch realized the woman who gave him life would lose hers this night.

All he could do the first few moments was stand there, a few feet away and look at her. He could feel mother's anxiety. He walked over and held her hand. It was cold so he smothered it with his warm, large hand. He kissed her forehead and told her he was sorry for all the suffering *he* had put her through. "I love you Mom and *always* will."

The racing heartbeat slowed as Mitch stroked his mother's face. Mom waited for her son to say goodbye. She was at peace.

Mitch kissed Mom's forehead one more time before he said goodbye. He could not watch her die. He thought he could. He could not. He wanted to be there with her, but something deep inside him knew his mother understood and it was okay to let go. "It's okay to leave me son, I was only waiting to say good-bye. I will be leaving this earth soon. I will always be with you. I love you, Mitchell."

Mitch walked out of the hospital room and quietly shut the door. He walked up to the nurses' station. It was late, just before 12:00 AM. The hospital was quiet, except for a few night nurses. One nurse asked how his mother was doing. Mitch said she would die soon. The nurse told him this could go on for days and … Mitch cut her off and said, "It *will not* go on for days! I know my mother and her suffering is almost over." Mitch's mother died an hour later.

Mom always said he was different. It wasn't until life was taken away, first from his father and now his mother that Mitch finally understood what she meant. Mom took part of him with her to the grave. Mitch was at an age where his vitality was diminishing, almost daily it seemed. Now, Mom was dead and he had no one to visit on Sundays. No one he could confide in. No one he could share his deepest sorrow. No one to say, "You're a good son." And no one to say, "I love you."

Mitch believed part of his soul would stay with hers until it was his time to die. Only *she* could hold on to it, until he found her and made sure she was safe. *Only then,* after knowing his dearest mother was at peace, could his entire soul be free. It was strange, part of him had questioned if God existed. Now that Dad and Mom were dead, Mitch *needed* God. Mom had been a faithful Catholic. Dad wasn't, but after he died she was left alone: *Alone,* to question her faith.

Mom felt betrayed by some of her children who refused to visit. She was lucky she came from a huge family. Most of her brothers were gone, but she did have several sisters who lived close and visited to tend to her needs. However, this was no substitute for her children. Children she needed after her husband died. She would often ask Mitch, "Why don't they come and visit me?"

"I don't know Mom, but I will not let you down nor will I let *anyone* harm you. I promise you mother. You can count on me."

"I know Mitchell, but can you tell me why my *own* children won't visit me?"

"I'm sorry, Mom, I really don't know. But it's not right, it's *not* right."

That was a lie. He did know, but did not have the heart to tell her. He couldn't tell Mom some of his siblings were so cold and selfish they could not find the time to visit their mother: A lonely old woman, dying slowly. *How* could he tell her that? Mitch loved Mom too much to shatter what was left of her heart. And there wasn't much left near the end.

MITCH DID NOT visit the coffee shop for over two months after Mother died. He didn't even drive by. When he did, he noticed from two blocks away something different. It was a bright sunny spring day when Mitch pulled in the coffee shop parking lot. "What in the hell did they do?!"

The coffee shop where Mitch spent one of the most significant days in his life had been converted into *a wine bar.* "You gotta' be kidding me," Mitch kept repeating. Kayla told Mitch one time the guy who owned the place was rich and didn't care if he kept it or not. Mitch never met him, but Kayla said he was fat, old, bald and mean—always smoked a fat cigar. Apparently, he decided to let the coffee shop go. What used to be dark brown siding was painted blood red. The coffee shop looked a little out of place, stuck between a salon and a drugstore. But it was real. There's just one word for this blood-red wine bar, *fake.* Mitch hated *anything* fake.

He decided to go inside and check it out. He got about ten yards from the front door and saw wine bottles resting on the ledges of the clear windows where the colored, stained-glassed one's used to be. He turned and walked back to his truck. The warm, inviting, cozy, coffee shop was gone.

THE YEARS WENT by and Mitch always wondered why he chose to walk into the coffee shop that Sunday. He wondered why he chose to disobey his mother's wishes and turn right when he should have turned left to go home. He wondered, but *never* regretted. Mitch was stubborn, like his mother and yet he somehow managed to do the right thing, like his father. Every morning when he looked in the mirror he could see his parents, his mortality.

What was Mitch's superpower? What was the *one* thing he did no one else had? The one thing no one else *could* do? It was being himself. It's the one thing—*the only thing* any of us can do. The lesson he learned from the friends he'd met that February 29th, in a leap year was to accept the life he had, and make it worth living.

BIBLIOGRAPHY

Chesbro, John Dwight, 1874-1931. Teams: Highlanders/Pirtes/RedSox 1899-1909. http://www.baseball-reference.com.

Lennon, John. *Give Peace A Chance*. Plastic Ono Band. Label, Apple, 1969.

Lennon, John. *Imagine*. Label, Apple, 1971.

ABOUT THE AUTHOR

Michael L. Eads loves the written word. He lives with his wife and dog near Seattle, Washington. He believes that: "New emotions are born from 'the process.' When individuals go through crisis and tragedy, unfamiliar feelings are summoned and our character is redefined. When we meet these challenges head on and accept the changes we must go through, we discover one more characteristic, integrity."

www.ingramcontent.com/pod-product-compliance
Lightning Source LLC
LaVergne TN
LVHW011226080426
835509LV00005B/348